TOKYO FROM VANCOUVER 2

Editor	George Wagner
Production Editor	Howard Kim
Design + Layout	Natalie Telewiak, David Zeibin, Aiden Callison, Howard Kim
Production	David Zeibin, Simon Montgomery, Mike Wartman, Jason Pare
Copy Editing	Christa Min, Graham Barron, Philippe Lew, Rebecca Bayer
Proof Reading	Christa Min, Jennifer Dee
Photo Editing	Howard Kim, David Zeibin
Cover Design	James Eidse
Published by	School of Architecture + Landscape Architecture
	Dr Raymond Cole, Director

University of British Columbia
402 – 6333 Memorial Road
Vancouver, British Columbia
V6T 1Z2 Canada

www.sala.ubc.ca

Printed in Canada by Hemlock Printers Ltd

TOKYO FROM VANCOUVER 2
ISBN 978-0-88865-662-9

TOKYO FROM VANCOUVER 2

TOKYO FROM VANCOUVER 2
UBC Architecture TOKYO 2006
www.tokyofromvancouver.com

Students   Ben Alexander, Graham Barron, Michael Barton, Rebecca Bayer,
Stella Boyland-Cheung, Aiden Callison, Kate Fretz, Mark George,
Howard Kim, Philippe Lew, Marsha Martin, Simon Montgomery,
Helen Ng, Jason Pare, Natalie Telewiak, Mike Wartman, David Zeibin

Faculty   George Wagner – *Director*, Atsushi Aiba, Souhei Imamura

Thanks   Fumio Matsumoto, Dana Buntrock, Sousuke Fujimoto, Kumiko Inui,
Mami Kikuchi, Sherry McKay, Ray Cole, Carolyn Pawluk, Yuko Shimizu,
Adam Silverman, David Stewart, Shunsuke Tabata, Ryuji Fujimura,
Yoshiharu Tsukamoto, Yasutaka Yoshimura

This publication was produced with the support of the LEF Foundation and
the Department of Architecture, University of British Columbia

CONTENTS

Thinking Type in TOKYO

GEORGE WAGNER

The American ornithologist John James Audubon (1785 – 1851) struggled to find a method that would allow him to realistically draw birds in lifelike poses. Simple field observation did not provide adequate time for careful drawing, and of course, birds move a lot. The answer was to shoot them — carefully. But when, in his studio, hanging them from one leg only intensified the lifeless aspect of the carcass, another method was required. His answer was to use wire, to thread it through the bird's body in such a way as to simulate a lifelike posture. Thus mounted, Audubon was able to proceed, and produce remarkable illustrations that suggest the speed and agility of the creatures they depict. It is a bit ironic that a lifelike representation would come at the cost of the life being represented.... as if to depict time, one must extinguish it.

In their field work, architects have often gravitated towards the city.... and this book documents the culture of one group that landed in Tokyo for four months. By its very nature, the city is indiscrete: continuous and open. Its form fosters movement, and so stimulates a mode of consciousness that privileges sight as the essential filter of classification and comprehension. These reactions are especially present among the illiterate — in this case those who can neither speak nor read Japanese, whose only point of leverage for their understanding is what they see. Looking at the city, what they often see is the fine grain of differences and similarities between things — scoping out a Darwinian logic that might explain the source of form and its repetition.

By the time I see my fifth rooftop driving range in Tokyo, I stop thinking so much about the driving range itself. Other questions arise: how are the other floors in the building used, and what kind of relation do they have to golf? What form of heraldry announces the range at the street? How are the two architectures, of mass and cage, connected? What is green, and what is not green? Towards what target do the golfers drive their balls — vista, void, sign, enclosure, projection? What relation exists between the 24 hours of the solar clock and the perfect, synthetic time of caged golf. Where does the rainwater go?

Many questions about the city lead away from its form, towards culture, economics and time. The time of architecture and of the city are quite different. It should be easy to argue that the ideal city, or worse, the eternal city, resonates most effectively as a marketing ploy rather than any description of a desired reality.

But architecture, on the other hand, is still very much conceived and understood in relation to ideals. Buildings need to operate as fixed, stable systems. Even those projects predicated on a fetishized mutability, like the Free University of Berlin, have survived as monuments to the idea without ever embodying the reality. The agent of change in architecture is usually personified as the individual — as opposed for instance, to the committee. A recent megastructure like Toyo Ito's Sendai Mediatheque has a superstructural system that allows the openness of the building's floorplate, without determining the finer grain of its occupation. What seems clear about the Mediatheque today is that neither the institutions that manage it, nor the individuals that use it, have control of the mechanisms that would allow the space to be occupied in a conscious way. It has slowly acquired the character of a temporary camp: part storage, part library.

The Mediatheque has already been designed, it just needs to be organized. These two verbs embody distinct ways of conceiving how buildings are formed, and how their occupation is qualified by time. Buildings are designed once, but can be organized and re-organized. What might an architecture look like in which an intense specificity is conceived not as an initial goal, but as a byproduct of occupation?

Much of the architecture shown in this book begins to answer that question. The heroic immediacy and scale of the central concrete column of Shinohara's House in Uehara is posed against a series of neutral and ordinary rooms. While the stacked units in Kumiko Inui's apartment 1 are roughly comparable, their occupation can only take the form of a daily improvisation. In contrast, Sou Fujimoto's work seems animated, and vaguely expressionistic — until one accepts the insistent seriality that ruthlessly measures each variation.

In outward appearance and general organization, Manabu Chiba's Platform might initially appear quite rigid. But the goal of the building's organization is quite qualitative, adhering to values of equity and difference. The apartments all share the same amenities, reaching from inside court to outside wall for ventilation. Balconies permit airing of laundry and futons. Bathrooms have windows. Spaces with less natural light available are compensated by increased volume. The intense rationalism of the whole confronts the deep humanity of the parts. If the form of the units vary, the values that determine their organization remain stable.

The subject is time. To offer his quarry eternity, the promise of a perfect representation, Audubon accepted the price of death. And maybe this is why architects should study closely a city like Tokyo. We cannot be sure what Tokyo looks like. It is always changing, and because its people are always moving, the city is never in one place. In response a schematic architecture has emerged, as available territory to be occupied, and reoccupied, until it isn't anymore.

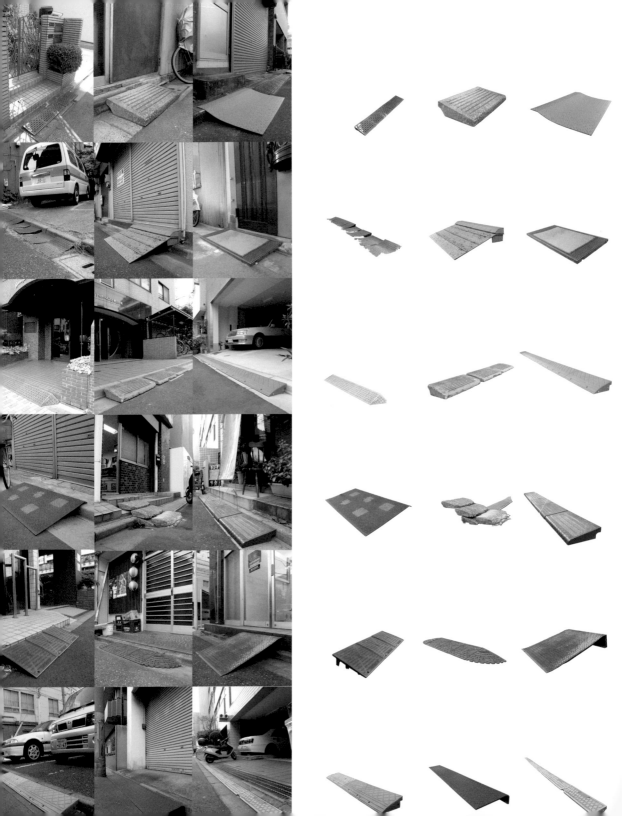

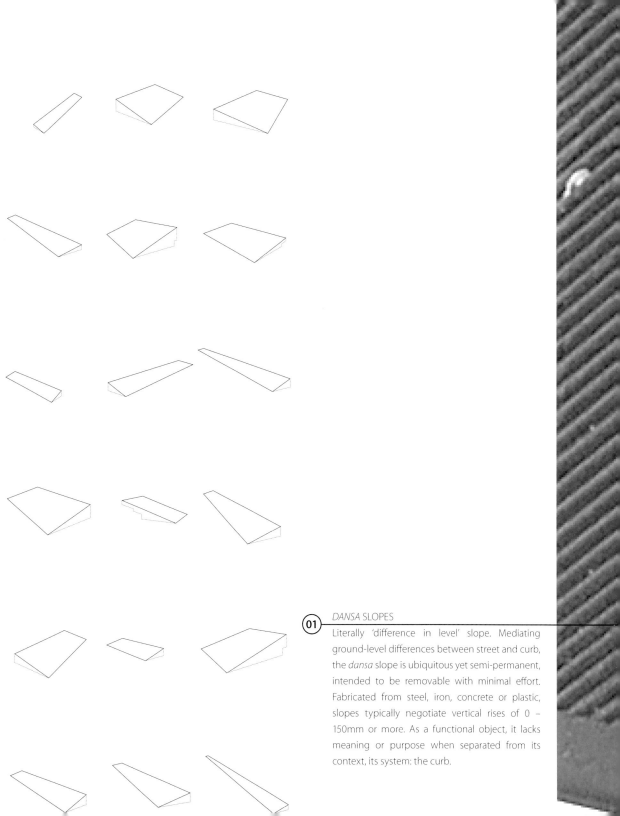

DANSA SLOPES

①①

Literally 'difference in level' slope. Mediating ground-level differences between street and curb, the *dansa* slope is ubiquitous yet semi-permanent, intended to be removable with minimal effort. Fabricated from steel, iron, concrete or plastic, slopes typically negotiate vertical rises of 0 – 150mm or more. As a functional object, it lacks meaning or purpose when separated from its context, its system: the curb.

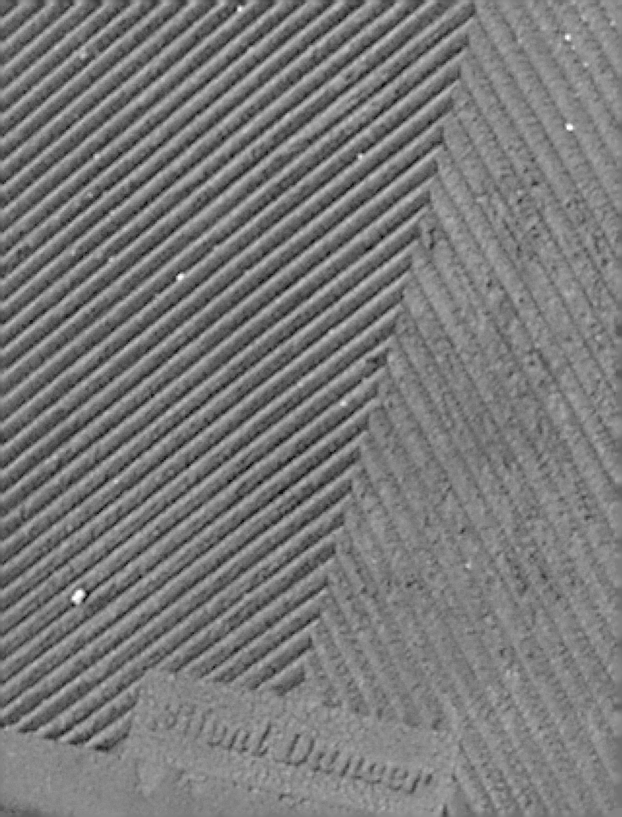

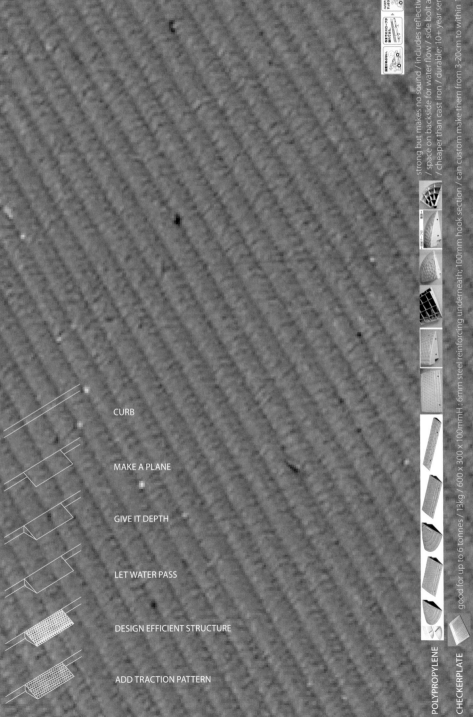

CURB

MAKE A PLANE

GIVE IT DEPTH

LET WATER PASS

DESIGN EFFICIENT STRUCTURE

ADD TRACTION PATTERN

FOR SALE

strong but makes no sound / includes reflective tape for night use / space on backside for water flow / side bolt attachment possible / cheaper than cast iron / durable; 10+ year service life / designed

POLYPROPYLENE

CHECKERPLATE   good for up to 6 tonnes / 13kg / 600 x 300 x 100mmH; 6mm steel reinforcing underneath; 100mm hook section / can custom make them from 3-20cm to within 1cm / ¥7500

CAST IRON   non-slip surface / painted to resist rust / 45mm height (¥5000) / 300x335x45mm / corner: 250x335x45mm / corner: 300x335x95mm / 100mm (¥5200) / 300x335x95mm / corner: 335x335x95

STEEL FRAME   can be used forever / good for locations with heavy snowfall / ¥5000 / galvanized, so it won't rust / good for ~2tonnes / 600 x 300 x 100mmH (25mm thick with 50mm hook section) / 10.9kg

INTERIOR

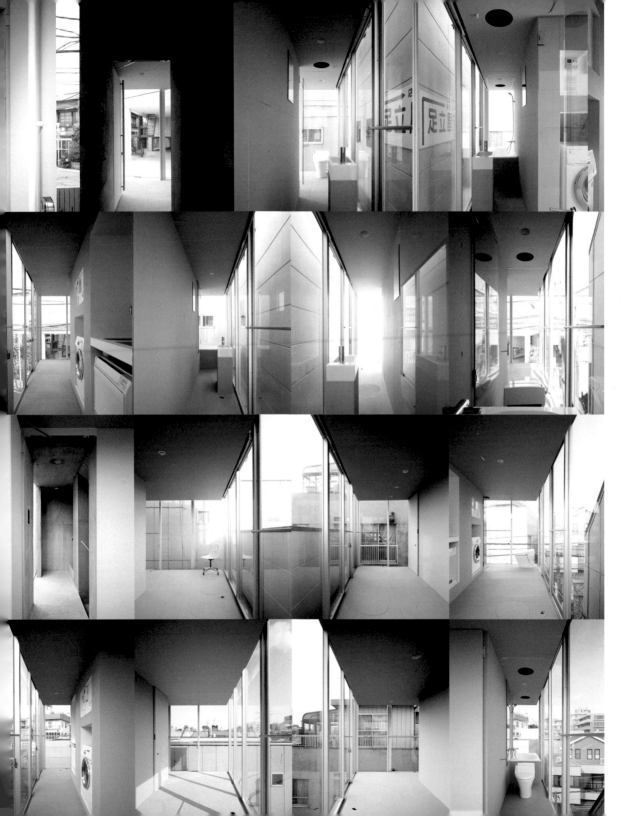

apartment I

KUMIKO INUI

Dior, Ginza

After starting my own practice in 2000, Office of Kumiko Inui, we received a number of commissions for storefronts and interior projects. The extent of these projects was always limited — to either interior spaces or exterior surfaces, but never extended to the design of whole buildings. Given these limitations, we deliberately focused our design ambitions on the production of discrete and local phenomenal effects, usually of the surface.

Phenomenal effects can exploit the uncertainty of what we perceive. If something looks strange, it might be because our perception cannot definitively process the artifact to produce a single, fixed reading. The moiré effect is one example of this kind of optical illusion. We see variations of the pattern because the resolution of our vision has limits. Our work has deliberately attempted to nurture visual ambiguity, and transfer those qualities into form. After realizing that our visual comprehension of the world can sometimes be uncertain, we have exploited that possibility to determine formal properties. We now study building design based on this hypothesis.

The **Louis Vuitton** store in Taipei is one of the projects where our design work was limited — in this case to the building's exterior. Taipei has a lush subtropical climate, with a myriad of trees lining its streets, and it was in response to their immediate presence at the site that we devised a strategy to camouflage the Vuitton store behind the vegetation. The facade is clad in a thin stone veneer, perforated with square holes and backlit. The holes, functioning individually like pixels, are aggregated into squares of differing size. They are orthogonal to, but not aligned with, a steel frame visible through the facade. The pattern is variegated and irregular, suggesting the silhouette — or shadow — of trees. Behind the trees, the facade recedes. At the same time, the underlying regularity of the holes' grid produces a static effect — a double reading oscillating between image and pattern. Such visual noise distinguishes

Louis Vuitton, Taipei

Shin-Yatsushiro surrounding landscape

Shin-Yatsushiro Monument

this facade in the urban landscape of Taipei.

meleze Gotemba, one of our favorite interior projects, is located in an outlet shopping mall that mimics a suburban American townscape while being set against the scenic backdrop of Mt. Fuji. Given the ironic situation of something so American in a setting so Japanese, we decided to take a delicate approach, avoiding the obviously sensational, for a subtler and dreamy effect. In the shop's interior we projected imaginary shadows based on the assumption of four distinct light sources and painted the projections in 20 different shades of the color Moth Green. All surfaces — the furniture and walls, (but not the ceiling and floor) — were caught in this crossfire of shadow. The overall effect was understated, provoking a slightly different dimension to everyday life, a subtle pulsation of light, only perceptible by the passage of time.

Shin-Yatsushiro Monument stands in front of a bullet train station, recently constructed in a rural landscape, where it looked isolated and out of place. We were commissioned to design a project that would celebrate the new station, but rather than directly address it, we chose to orient the monument to the surrounding rural landscape by giving it the scale and iconography of the local houses. The walls of the hollow monument were perforated by square holes of widely varying dimension. From a distance only the larger holes were visible, so it looked like an ordinary house with windows. On approach, the smaller holes become visible, until finally, standing before the monument, you read that it is hollow and its surface completely perforated. What seemed familiar now appears both finely scaled and immaterial.

house K is a house for two male fashion designers who required a residence with an organization slightly different from the standard single-family house. They wanted individual and equivalent bedrooms and bathrooms. They were not interested in having a common living space as the centerpiece of the house, stating that they would visit each other's rooms should they want to share time and space. Furthermore, they suggested that one of them might soon move out of the house, and a friend would take over their room. At best, the domestic arrangement was uncertain and suggested something like a non-hierarchical hybrid of single-family house, apartment, and dormitory. We were interested in such an ambiguous program. Our ambition then, was to

Outlet shopping mall seen against Mt. Fuji

meleze Gotemba

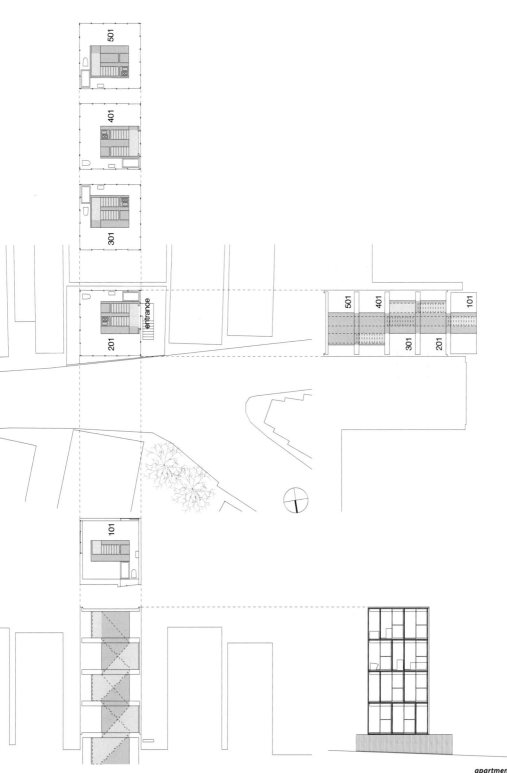

apartment I, plan and section

imagine an architecture as weak as possible, one that would not strictly specify how the house would be inhabited. In other words, we tried to make very flexible architecture.

When we studied **apartment 1** we had the opportunity to further focus on the ambiguity of the domestic program. There are five units in this apartment building sited in Hiroo and each unit, which occupies one floor, is only 20 square metres. In Japan, apartment buildings with extremely small one-room apartments are common and usually disliked by the neighborhood for importing dens of noisy and ill mannered youth. As a building type, one room apartments (also known as mansions), are often a jarring intrusion into landscapes of small houses, organized as they are with small cells arranged along exterior single-loaded corridors. Poor construction and crowding compromise further the privacy of the living units, which provide nothing more than the minimum that is necessary in the housing markets. I personally do not want to make such unhappy buildings. However, for practical and economic reasons, the production of such buildings will never stop. Our challenge was to avoid perpetuating the inherently negative aspects of this building type.

Because the building is organized vertically, the design of the stair became critical, and as its space needed to be minimized, there is no landing between floors. The position of the staircase at each floor is shifted, producing a different apartment plan. From the street this variation is visible and it's possible to read the building as a single-family house. In this project we try to break the formal stereotype of the one room mansion. At the same time, with the plan of each apartment organized around the shifting central stair, we have attempted to develop new possibilities in the organization of the domestic program.

Until recently, ambiguity within the context of architectural design has meant the change of functional program over time. I am not interested in such ambiguity. I am interested in the ambiguity that occurs here and now. Being sensitive to what is happening in the present, I would like to renovate architectural design a little. I am hoping that these studies of the potential of storefront and interior projects have developed my ability to perceive and encourage delicate conditions around our world.

house K

501

401

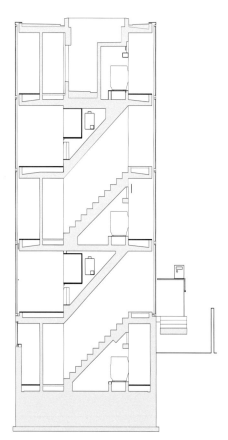

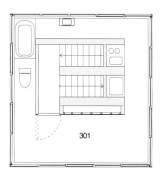

301

201

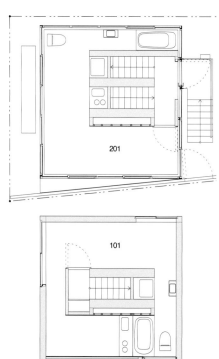

101

apartment I, detailed plan and section

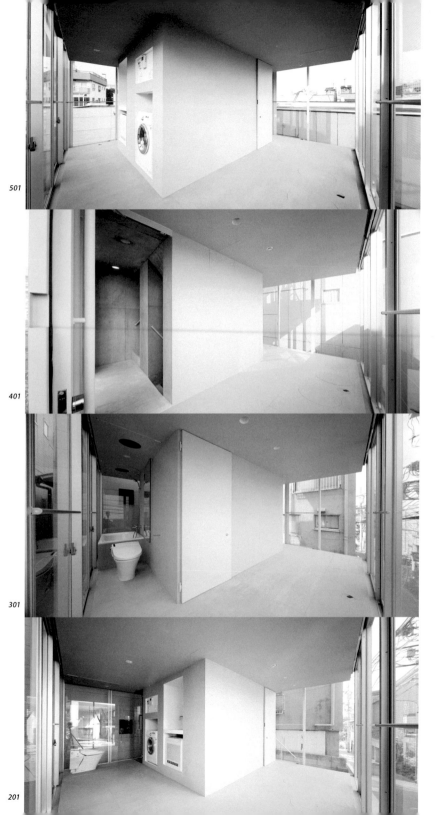

501

401

301

201

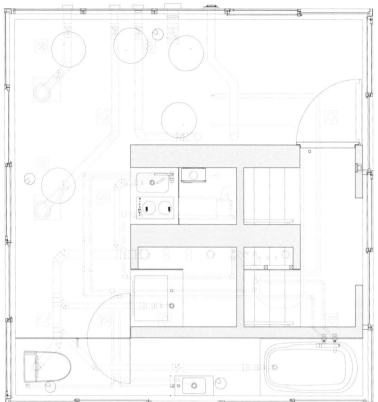

401, building services overlay plan

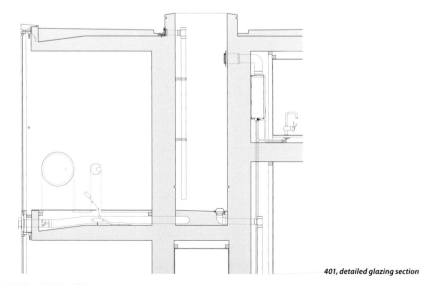

401, detailed glazing section

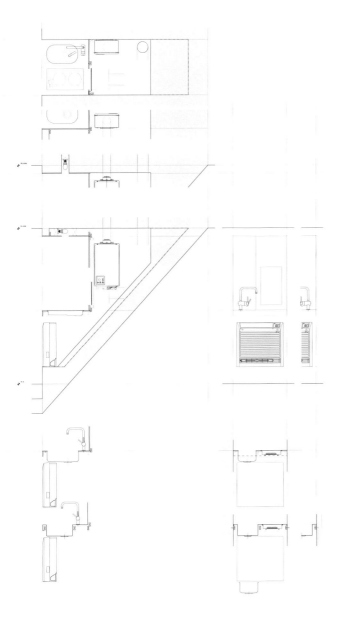

detailed kitchen section

apartment I

GEORGE WAGNER

One room mansions, ironically named, motel scaled apartment houses, provide one of the irreducible increments of Japanese urbanism: minimal dwelling units of around 20 square metres. These apartments are little more than staging areas, launch platforms for lives sustained in the space of the surrounding city. As Akira Suzuki has well discussed, the ubiquity of convenience stores and their broad array of products relieves the one room apartment of any productive dimension.[1] Not a miniaturization of anything grander, these units are ultimately schematic — a prefabricated plastic bathroom, minimal kitchen, with the balance of space available to accept the daily rituals of private life and its accumulations.

The mansions are often seen as a scourge by their neighbours who lament the increased density, itinerant population, and barracks style they bring to residential quarters. Typologically, their organization is quite standardized: one or two stories, with a single loaded exterior corridor. To say that the mansion is highly reduced and distilled in its form might hint at a rationalist rigour that is always absent: imagine a metal dog kennel with Regency doors, and pipes and AC units appended. At the same time, these buildings form a growing market and offer lucrative investments for buyers of individual units, especially given the redistribution of Japan's population to urban centers.

Kumiko Inui's apartment 1 in Hiroo is strongly planted within the pejorative cultural context of the one room mansion. But as a work of architecture, it does not begin there, and one significant reason is because the small site has forced a vertical organization of the units. The 5 apartments, each 20 square metres, are stacked vertically, accessed through a shifting concrete stair tower from which they are also cantilevered. On each floor, the building's perimeter is divided into five single glazed panels, operable windows that span from floor to ceiling. By its proportions, this mansion is a tower. But unlike the arrangement of the generic office towers it surreally resembles in which perimeter and core ascend concentrically, Inui strategically shifts the core's position on each floor, rendering each apartment subtly distinct.

The living space of the apartments occupies an irregular margin, never more than 1.8 metres deep between the building's core and perimeter glazing. The core's mass absorbs a small kitchenette unit and clothes washer. Mechanical systems have been meticulously concealed within the concrete structure, and the juncture of the floor system and exterior wall is detailed to receive, and thus conceal, the Venetian blinds that are essential for privacy.

Released into the singular space of the apartment are a sink, a bathtub, and a toilet, positioned so as to foster programmatic adjacency, even if access between fixtures is sometimes difficult. In each unit, the closest dimension of the core to the exterior glazing is exactly determined by the width of the bathtub — blocking circulation, and so inflecting the way that each space is used. The bathroom fixtures' role is poignant, given the ubiquity of the prefabricated plastic bathroom in postwar Japanese housing. Inui literally explodes this precedent, so that the bathroom fixtures become the only discrete and fixed elements within the unit's open space. The result is surreal — Duchamp's *Fountain* only suggests the effect.

The domestic space of Kumiko Inui's apartment 1 is fully liminal, in the truest and most provocative sense of the word. This is the space between inside and outside, both psychologically and metaphysically. The warhorse binary of public/private is not useful, not because these states are not available in the project — they are — but because they cannot fully describe the reality, and the realism of Inui's space: in the city, but not of it. This is a domestic interior, but it is not the womb, a safe and complete enclosure. The units at apartment 1 fully possess many of the shortcomings one would associate with the mansion type — the determinist reduction of domestic life to the simplest notation, for instance, but they intensely clarify for the viewer, and one must assume for the occupant as well, what quantity it is that constitutes a home.

mansion, Futako Tamagawa

[1]Akira Suzuki, *Do Android Crows Fly Over the Skies of an Electronic Tokyo?* Architectural Association, London 2001, pp. 16-33.

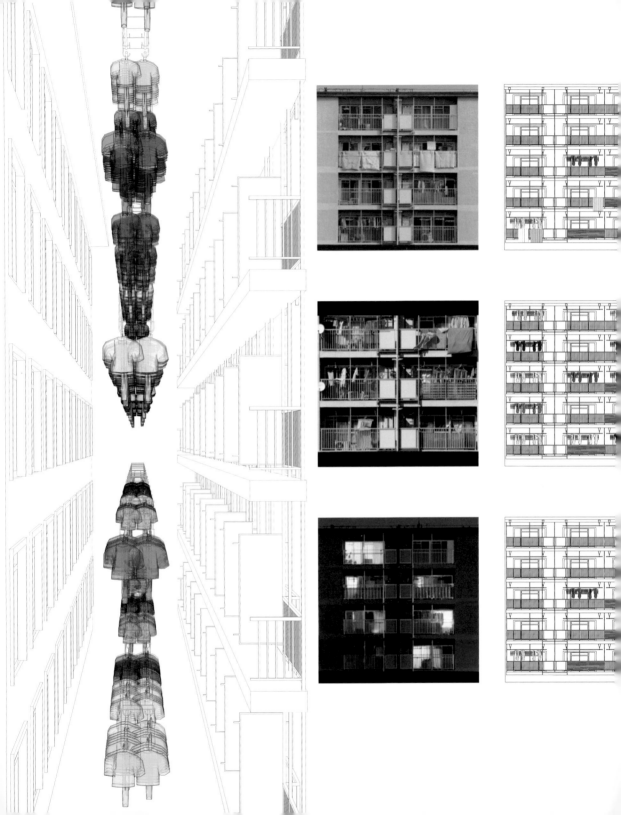

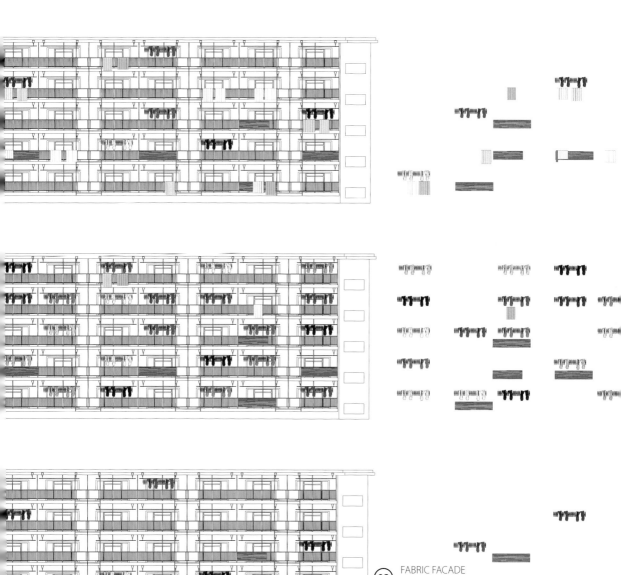

FABRIC FACADE

02 Balconies, 0.9m in depth, are active extensions of the domestic realm that give the facade depth and variation through a dense layering of textiles. These individual pieces of clothing, bedding, and grass screens contribute to a collective accumulation of textiles that resonate at the scale of the building to create a fabric facade that is constantly changing, reflecting the daily activities of the collective occupation as they relate to the time of day.

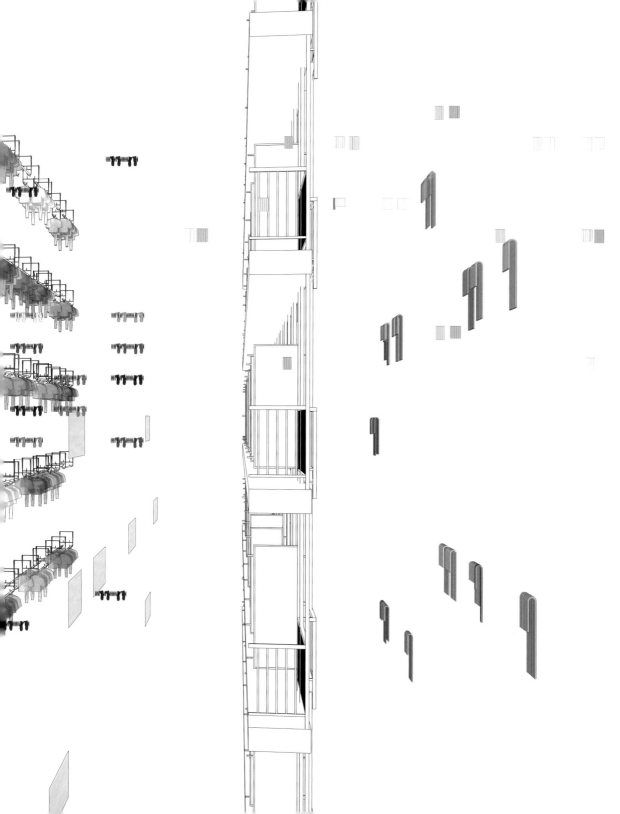

01

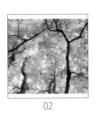

02

03

04

05

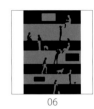

06

07

08

09

10

11

12

13

14

15

16

17

18

19

20

21

22

23

24

25

26

27

28

29

30

7[+1] Works

SOU FUJIMOTO

22 NOVEMBER 2006

Today I am going to show you eight projects, ranging in scale from a small house to a large facility for children.

First of all, I will give you three key phrases:

Between nature and artifice

Formless form

Local relations

I think these three keywords have the same meaning. But I would like to say the same thing by different phrases.

It might be a little abstract, but I think it will help you understand my work.

In a single phrase: ambiguity emerging from clear new geometry.

PRIMITIVE FUTURE HOUSE, 2004

[img. 1]

The first project is named "primitive future house." This house is derived from a completely new concept. In this project, I intended to combine furniture, architecture, and landscape in order to create a new standard of architecture. "Local relation" is the keyword.

[img. 2]

Let's take a forest for example. The forest has no big rules, but it is made from small rules of relationships between one tree and other trees. These small rules create the whole forest. And if you were to make architecture the same way the forest is made, it would have fantastic spaces — very simple and also very complex. In my projects I am trying to develop an emergent order, coming from the bottom up instead of the top down.

[img. 3]

This is a house. Thinking about architecture, a large flat floor is a big rule, a top down order. I would like to defeat the floor. So I tried to divide the floor and connect it again with an interval of 35cm.

On the one hand, this interval relates to the size of the human body. 35cm is the height we can sit on, while 70cm — the double of 35cm — is the height of a desk, as in this picture. So these slabs can be used as chairs, desks, floors, roofs, shelves, stairs, lighting, openings, gardens, and of course as structure. Functions emerge in these relative fields of slabs in relation to a person's position or posture. A desk for one person is a floor for another. A shelf for someone is a chair for someone else.

On the other hand, the whole was devised as a topography without specific function.

We can say it is a relative field without particular function. People can find various functions by instinct in this topography.

Layers of slabs are also the system of structure. I divided pillars, too. And all we have to do is connect layers of slabs together, one by one, vertically, with a thin truss. As a result of that process, in spite of its strange cloud like shape, this house has a coherent structure. Fundamental elements of architecture, space, furniture, and structure are integrated in this new form.

Take the Maison Domino by Le Corbusier, one of the most impressive drawings of all Modernism. It has a certain beauty as pure archetype. In this drawing, fundamental elements of architecture — floor, piloti, and stair — are all clearly defined. Each of these elements is distinguished from the others, and its role clearly defined. The Domino has a machine-like beauty, in which all the components are precisely assembled according to a big rule. Yes, this machine is a system of big orders.

[img. 4]

Instead, I inverted what Le Corbusier did. All those components, such as floors, pillars, and stairs, fuse into one composition without individual distinction. We can say it's simpler than Domino. Though its whole appearance is complicated, the method is very simple and clear. Domino and primitive future house look completely different, but both of them suggest primitive archetypes of the house. They are treating the basic field of our life in different ways — one is artificial, the other is between nature and artifice.

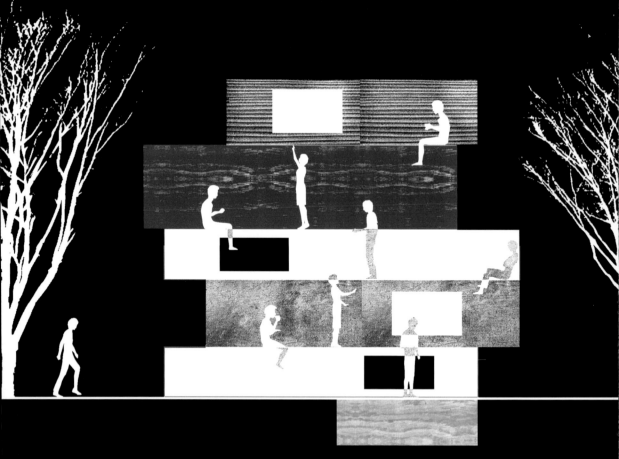

ATELIER

[img. 5]

We can often adapt one idea to other projects. This project is an atelier for my brother, who is a painter. The programmatic elements include a warehouse, a garage, a living room, an atelier, and a bathroom.

What I had in mind was to generate a space that is not a nest but a cave. I think a nest is functionally made to satisfy the needs of the inhabitant. The most direct expression of this quality is probably the way space between floor and ceiling is calibrated to fit our bodies. On the other hand, a cave is already there and not made to fit a dweller. But it gives us a chance to exploit the specificity of a pre-existing space or invent functions in adaptation of particularity. It is a landform of possibilities. The cave has richer spaces than the nest. But is it possible to invent an artificial method to create a cave?

This house has five stories, though you can see the vertical dimension between each floor — half normal height — is much lower than usual. But

don't worry about hitting your head. When two floors are connected there is adequate height, and some of the slabs are carved to produce spaces where we can stand straight up.

The bedroom in the house, with its low ceiling height, suggests the space of a cave. It is like bivouacking in a mountain and finding a small space to creep into. These spaces, indeterminate programmatically, become available for various improvisations of daily life.

[img. 6]

In this drawing, the lower half of our body is in the gray layer, while the upper half is in the black layer. It seems half fitting to us and half not-fitting to us. Space and man can be combined in mutual relations. We can use the cozy spaces of gaps between these small floors in multiple ways. As a result of this simple operation of dividing floors into two, and sticking them together again, I think I can produce more richness than before. In this new equation ½ + ½ > 1.

[img. 7]

In this project I tried to create a space of no intention through an intentionally precise design method. I think it's not interesting any more to plan everything with a predetermined architectural intention, and for spaces then to be used only as intended. Rather, I like the idea of things growing through a natural process, of form being achieved anonymously, over time, like forests or old cities. I'd like to create architecture the same way.

T HOUSE

[img. 8]

This is a house for a family of four, realized in a calm residential area. The house, in a sense, is a one room space, with many branches outward. These branches include a bedroom for parents, a living room, a kitchen, a study, a piano room, a Japanese-style room, a bathroom, and two rooms for children. At the same time, all of them form one interconnected room of very unique shape.

[img. 9]

Usually, a house is divided strictly by walls and doors into rooms, like a bedroom or a living room. In such cases, we have no choice but to enter a room or leave it — 0 or 1. But I think there could be more sensitive gradations of space between a bedroom and a living room. For example, you can find a reclusive area deep inside the private room, or a territory near to the living room though inside the private room, or a zone almost out of the private room — various gradations that are much richer than the opposites of inside or outside.

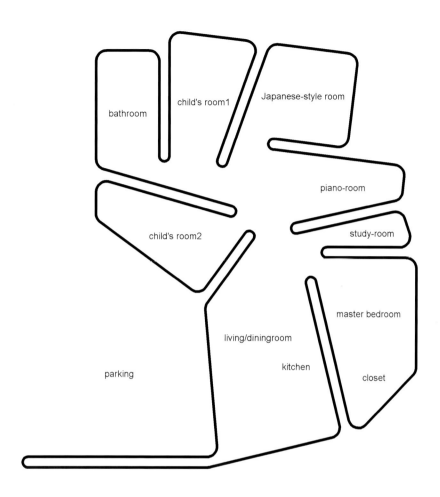

labels in image: bathroom, child's room1, Japanese-style room, piano-room, child's room2, study-room, master bedroom, living/diningroom, kitchen, closet, parking

[img. 10]

Dividing the house into rooms might preclude such a spatial gradation. So I was eager to represent all the infinite irrational numbers between 0 and 1 as a space in a house, not just 0 or 1. That's how this plan was born.

In this house, when you sit deep in one of these branches, you may feel very comfortable surrounded by these walls, but when you stand up and start to walk to the bathroom, say, the spaces around you spread out and various new scenes appear, bypassing the walls. Walking around in this house is an unexpected, fresh experience. It's so amazing that by just a few steps, one can experience such a dramatic and rich change of sight and scenery.

[img. 11]

Put another way, this house bears some similarity to a traditional Japanese garden and its alleys. Stepping stones are usually placed at those alleyways, and the scenery changes as people step from stone to stone. Each step renews the relationships of the things around. Here is a picture taken from a Japanese-style room toward a living room. Seeing these pictures, it is easy to understand the fact that a variety of spaces are combined, even in one room. From this viewpoint, even though some spaces are hidden by the walls, they are nonetheless connected and share an atmosphere.

[img. 12]

In this house one of the biggest objectives was to produce a sense of distance from the world. I think a house should be a field of distance. Privacy in a house means a distance of far-apart; either next to each other but unseen, or very far but directly seen — half connected, half divided. There are various distances in any house. The shape of the plan could create such a distance in a very simple way, by means of a single stroke drawing.

ANNAKA ART FORUM

[img. 13]

This project won an international competition in 2003. It is located at the center of the new town, a multi-purpose facility, and I think of it as an architectural urban square where people can gather and do various things independently, or sometimes interdependently. Here I proposed a single 7,000 square metre room of unique shape. This is the space of *half-divided/half-connected*. This shape creates a range of scales, from an intimate semi-enclosed space to a larger wide open space that can extend beyond itself.

[img. 14]
Users can select a space to fit the scale of their activities. The space of
half-divided/half-connected allows for simultaneous activities to occur in close
proximity or within distant view. Even at a distance all activities within the space
become interdependent and exert a mutual influence on one another.

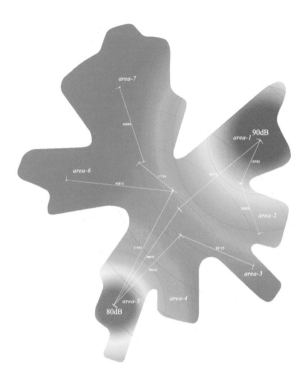

: ATTENUATION OF SOUND

Injurtt : Mac0803.trt
Doyot : Mac0803.txt
Focus : 55.400 65.900 4.000
C.L.=8.000   S=7000.000
Dfact : 1000.000
Mfacty : 0.5000

30.00   100.00

ATTENUATION OF SOUND*   *The full diagram serves as a check list to
encourage optimisation of sustainability, prompt innovative thinking , and inform decision making throughout
all stages of design and development.

[img. 15]

    In this project, as in T house, the whole is given form only as the summation of organic local relations. Organic relations means the exact opposite of the machine. For example, in this project one can never take a certain area away from others because that area has meaning only when connected to others. No area exists independently. That's the important difference between this plan and a normal multi-room plan. Independence is provided only by interdependence. And I believe these kind of mutual relations may suggest some possibilities for a new architecture.

Aria mit verschiedenen Veränderungen
BWV 988

Johann Sebastian Bach
1685-1750

BACH

[img. 16]

Here I am going to compare the space of Mies van der Rohe to the space I am pursuing in work. This is a score from Bach's beautiful piano music. I think the system of this score displays some elemental attributes of modernism. In this score, you can see the lines. These lines represent the homogeneous stream of time. This stream of time is a basic framework, a dominant, absolute framework; we lay out each note on it in order to script music. It is in exactly the same way as this, that Mies suggested the grid pattern as the premise for the homogeneous space of modernism.

Aria mit verschiedenen Veränderungen
BWV 988

Johann Sebastian Bach
1685-1750

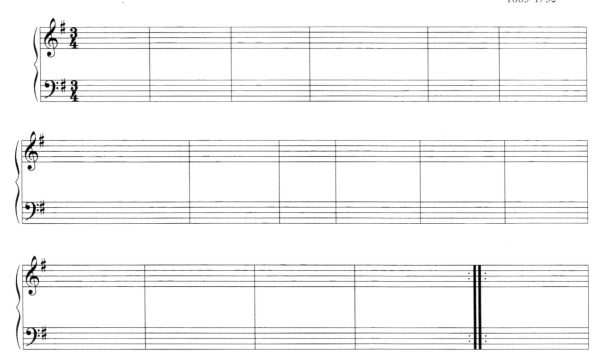

[img. 17]

This is Mies. All the notes have vanished. What makes him great is that he suggested such a homogeneous flow of time, a homogeneous grid pattern that can be architecture by itself. But then after Mies, what can we do on this earth? Whatever we might do, we can never compete with Mies because he has already realized such an essential reduction of architectural possibility. We are left to dance on the field made by Mies. All the more reason for us to think deeply of what we can do to go beyond the framework of Mies.

Aria mit verschiedenen Veränderungen
BWV 988

Aria

Johann Sebastian Bach
1685-1750

[img. 18]

   This I think is something new. The bars have vanished and now the various notes are floating. Unlike Mies, I have tried to erase that homogeneous flow of time. In the ordinary score, homogeneous time is given in advance, and after that the notes are placed. Instead, in this new score, time starts to flow just when the note starts to sound. There is no homogeneous flow of time. Each note has its own time, and it is the sequence of these various times that creates the order. So only in the relations of each note to another does the flow of time exist. This is the principle of bottom-up order, or the order of local relations. Homogeneous time is a big order. If we can think of space the way we think of time, I believe there are new possibilities for architecture, the architecture we can imagine.

DORMITORY

[img. 19]

This dormitory is part of a rehabilitation facility for mentally disabled people that helps them gradually readapt to society after release from the hospital. Fundamental ambiguity was required here, for the facility to be both a comfortable *home* for each of the twenty residents, while being a social, city-like place of diversity.

[img. 20]

This is a diagram of its plan. Squares of the same size are aligned, and the connection adjusted to various angles. So at first sight their placement seems disorderly. But in fact they have merely a simple order that dictates only that these squares may only join at a corner. I am interested in this relation of adjacency, in other words, the phenomenon of local relations. In nature we often find examples of the kind of spaces I call local relations. Thinking about a forest again, a tree cannot affect the whole forest, it just stands and grows according to the size and distance of neighbouring trees. Nevertheless, a forest has some loose kind of order as a whole. Such a wonder in nature motivated me to create an architecture with similar qualities.

[img. 21]

Through this project, particularly in planning a cozy space such as this alcove, I found the possibility of a "space of no intention." I admire the book *Architecture Without Architects* by Bernard Rudolfsky. I like the old cities created anonymously in that book. But now I am an architect, and I wanted to create my own "architecture without architects." It's a bit like creating a cave by an artificial method, and I think the bottom-up method is one of the ways to accomplish that.

TREATMENT CENTER FOR MENTALLY DISTURBED CHILDREN

[img. 22]

This is a treatment center for mentally disturbed children where they live together to regain their mental health.

[img. 23]

This is the plan. I have hoped it would be possible to make a building with a random method, as if its elements merely scattered, and that the result would be a dreamlike building. These boxes of 6.3m by 6.3m were scattered without planning. You can imagine it looks like the Bach score without the lines. As I was working on this plan, I gradually found that the method of randomness could become a strong rule for making a space. Because of the randomness, we can develop the plan as precisely as possible, adjusting the boxes in correspondence with the complicated program.

However, the amazing point of this method goes beyond that. In spite of the fact that we worked on the composition very carefully, the space created still looks unplanned, without specific intention. That paradox, the gap between a process and its result, is very interesting for me.

[img. 24]

In brief, even after a deliberate process, the spaces take form as if designed with no intention at all. Irregular alcoves are produced between the scattered boxes. Although the spaces have no function, children can play with the place, interpreting the landscape freely and living very well in it.

[img. 25]

The children can choose the scale and brightness of an alcove to stay and hide in, improvising their use of this space and its many corners. In this project the building's spaces never force certain functions on people, instead inspiring them to invent use by following their instincts.

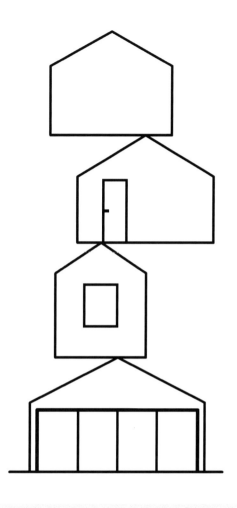

TOKYO APARTMENT

[img. 26]

This last project is small, charming, strange, exciting. The key words are: "no relation."

[img. 27]

This is a project of collective housing in a crowded residential section of Tokyo. I named it "Tokyo Apartment" because the project is inspired by and represents the emerging order of a complicated city like Tokyo.

The concept, as you see, is very clear: piling up the houses. It consists of five dwelling units, including the owner's. Each dwelling unit is made of two or three independent rooms of prototypical, "house-like" shapes. Some of the rooms of the apartments move beyond the discrete house form. For example one room might be on the ground floor and the other on the second floor. In these cases, rooms are connected by outside stairs.

It could be said that each dwelling unit is realized by the experience of the city as well as by the interior character of the rooms. When you climb the external stairs, you will have an experience of climbing up a big mountain made of city parts.

To access the upstairs, you might climb a roof as well as take the stairs. It's interesting that to get home you have to step on the roof of someone else's house. That will give inhabitants a chance to walk over roofs as if they were flying freely over the city. They experience the city three-dimensionally. I would say that if you live in this house then you are the owner of a small city.

[img. 28]

It's rare in architecture to pile things that have no relation to each other. On the contrary, I think "no relation" can produce some new richness. A new kind of continuity with no relation exists here. A complex and seemingly random situation is made into one simple form.

No relation does not mean there is no relation. I think there is a relation named "no relation." You might also call it a "one-by-one order." One-by-one is the system by which the forest is made. So this theme of no relation has something to do with the state of the random cubes I mentioned in the former project. Those projects are completely artificial things, but the experience of the space has some quality beyond the artificial. It is my hope that at this point we have arrived at strategies that will allow us to make a space like a cave, maybe a transparent conceptual cave, by an artificial method.

Aria mit verschiedenen Veränderungen
BWV 988

Johann Sebastian Bach
1685-1750

Aria

[img. 18] again

Now, at the end of my lecture, I show you again the Bach score with no lines. I think it represents some new quality of space. It will open the possibility for a new coordinate system beyond the grid order, and yet it retains simplicity — that was Mies's achievement. And so, I think it is very exciting.

Today's works are the first few steps of a long vision towards a new architecture.

Thank you very much.

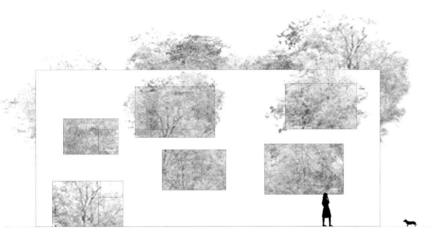

HOUSE N

[img. 29 & img. 30]

img. 29 and img. 30 are from my newest project named "House N" in Oita, Japan.

DISCUSSION

Ben Alexander: You spoke about how some modernist architecture has influenced your thinking, and you mentioned Le Corbusier and Mies. But in some of your projects, particularly the teahouse and the children's dormitory, you talked about gradations of occupation, of half-divided and half-connected space. At one point you made comparisons to the Japanese garden and teahouse. I wonder how traditional Japanese architecture has influenced your design work, or if it has? It seems that some of the ideas are quite the same while the form is clearly different.

Sou Fujimoto: To tell the truth, I am not such a specialist in traditional Japanese architecture, or in traditional Japanese thinking, but there are some aspects of our historical culture I find very interesting. For instance, the score of Bach that I showed is inspired by a famous contemporary Japanese composer, Toru Takamitsu, who died a few years ago. He studied traditional Japanese music and also wrote books about Japanese gardens. I think it's the biggest influence for me. Traditional Japanese thinking comes from the garden: the Japanese garden has no big rooms. But if you walk inside the Japanese garden you can see very clear intentions between one step and the next step. New scenes and landscapes unfold with each pace. It is very complex but very rich. Because if a landscape is dominated by a big order, a big view, or a great wonder, one or two or three steps is never really enough to change the scene, and you are always aware of the power of the big move above all. But when elements change you start to think in terms of the multiple relations between many things, and then your own step is the thing that changes the situation. Similar conditions exist in traditional building. Japanese music traditionally has no conductor — three or four people will play their instruments together. If one changes their tempo, it changes the music, and so the music itself is a condition of their specific relation while playing. It is a typical quality of traditional Japanese culture. But now Japan is not so traditional, but very modern. I am hoping that I can use my body to understand this tradition. That is the current focus of my study.

Souhei Imamura: You spoke about formless form, of architecture without architects. These are inherently contradictory ideas, and it could be very easy to make relations to the principles of Zen. Not only because he looks like a monk!

Sou Fujimoto: A monk with a smoke!

Souhei Imamura: Maybe I can ask you, because maybe, when you are in these lecture situations, and you are from Japan, people will ask you these kinds of things. The impression of the lecture is different from the last time I saw you speak. Usually it is not so straightforward. It was very clear today, in English. But Fujimoto is saying something very unclear; the ideas themselves are quite complex. He wants to make a very soft system, but using very strong stuff, strong materials. And these are contradictory impulses. And so he tries to clarify what he is doing. One of the problems in invoking archaic Japanese tradition is that it is kind of full of dead concepts. So I can move this book here and I can move that book there, and place them in specific relation, but I cannot explain why, or what exactly that relation means. That is what has happened, and these are the kinds of weaknesses that exist in our philosophy. So we just say: go to a Zen garden and you will see it, but I cannot explain. That is what has happened. But to go back to Fujimoto's work, he speaks of formless form, and contradiction, but what he is showing — the design itself is very clear and articulate.

Mark George: At the beginning you made the statement that there are more fairly small rules in the forest than there are large rules, and that seems like a metaphor for all this work. In the mental health campus you showed, you used an element of chaos, of random disorder and then attempted to bring to it a very considered order in the plans. It seems like a strategy that could be very productive to the development of ideas about both program and site. So it made me wonder if you have worked in an urban condition, and what the context was of the projects you showed towards the end of the lecture.

Sou Fujimoto: I was born Hokkaido in the Northern part of Japan, in a place where there was nothing....

Souhei Imamura: Hokkaido is the only part of Japan where you can see the horizon.

Sou Fujimoto: The first three or four projects I showed happened to be in Hokkaido, where there was nothing around, so I had to think only about my architecture, to create some quality just from my architecture. These days I have to work in other contexts, but the manner of my thinking is not so changed. I do not think so much about a response to context, but to create some new quality that can influence the surroundings. The intention is not to get something, but to give something. I think its more exciting, but it does not mean to ignore the context, but to see the context — and then think what to do, and consider how it can be made a little better. But, to tell the truth, there is no realized architecture because I have not built anything in Tokyo yet. This apartment, the last project I showed, is my first challenge with how to deal with Tokyo. It's a little... [he looks at Imamura, who puts his hands in fists and moves them together so as to suggest pushy or tough. Fujimoto repeats Imamura's gesture.] Yes, I know. But I enjoy this project and will work very hard to realize this.

Souhei Imamura: Mark, if you bring this project to the studio, maybe George would say, hey, go back home and rethink this, okay. But Fujimoto here has actually realized it, which is a bit different. It's a good point because Fujimoto started his career in Hokkaido and that is a very particular landscape. It's a bit like the situation of a Dutch architect starting his or her practice on reclaimed land: it's very difficult to make something first, on no man's land, where your building might inevitably have to be autonomous. It's a good comparison to Tsukamoto's work. We recently visited his house. Tsukamoto is a kind of city boy. Fujimoto here, he is a Hokkaido boy.... He always needs to think his project in calculation to other things, or somehow, he cannot survive.

Mike Wartman: Could you say that many of your ideas have developed from being in Tokyo? When you were speaking of architecture without architects, it made me think of Tokyo as the city without a planner, with the kind of buildup of relations between things over time that you were speaking of.

Sou Fujimoto: I like Tokyo very, very much. I was born in Hokkaido and moved to Tokyo for university at 18 years old, and it was a very, very shocking experience for me. Because in Hokkaido you have nothing, and the road is as straight as straight, to the horizon. In Tokyo your first impression is of very big buildings. But when I started to live in Tokyo, the small buildings and small alleys and roads were very comfortable to me. It's just like you walk out of the house but are surrounded by some other house — in the city, but in a house. It's very comfortable. I think it's very good. But back in Hokkaido after a stay in Tokyo, Hokkaido seems very strict, very dangerous. It's wide open. There is nothing to protect me. There are big contrasts between the two.

Souhei Imamura: Hokkaido is somehow similar to American cities: developed after the war, a regular grid, familiar, typical, artificial....

Sou Fujimoto: Tokyo, with its winding roads of indistinct origin, does not seem artificial.

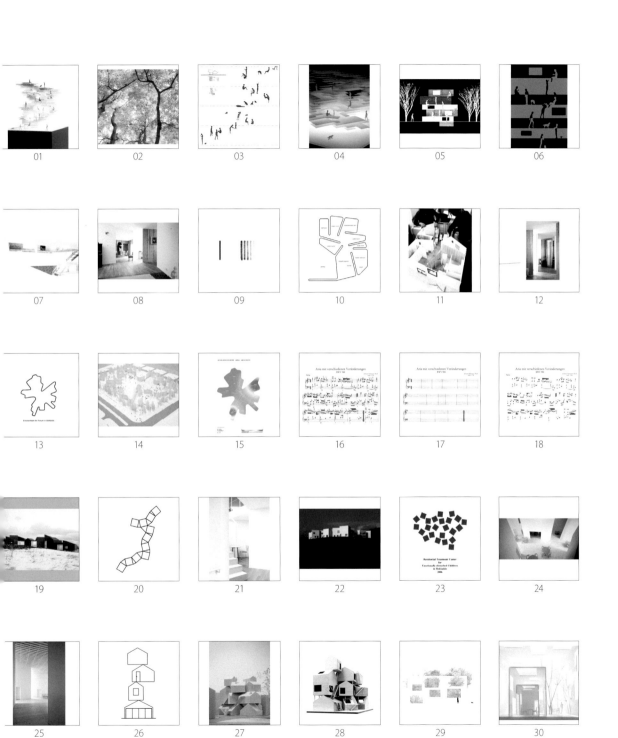

01

02

03

04

05

06

07

08

09

10

11

12

13

14

15

16

17

18

19

20

21

22

23

24

25

26

27

28

29

30

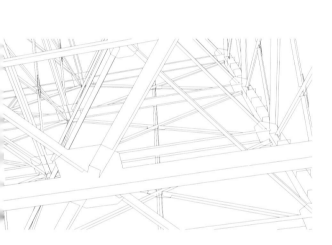

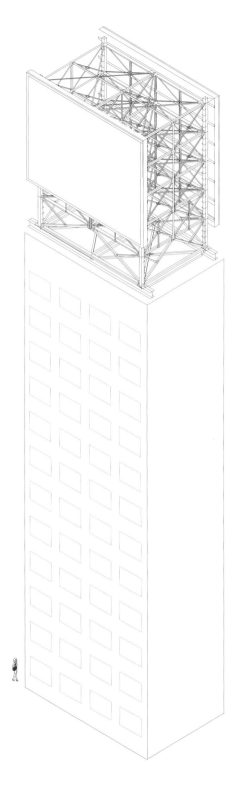

HIGH SIGN STRUCTURES  ⟨03⟩

Building regulations in Tokyo specify the maximum occupiable space permitted. They also allow for an unoccupiable element at the building's top that can be used for mechanical systems or signage. Designed to support the signage, open structures fabricated of steel sections create unoccupied space locked within a field of structural components. Structural organization varies and is dependent on size of steel sections, orientation and size of sign, and plan geometry.

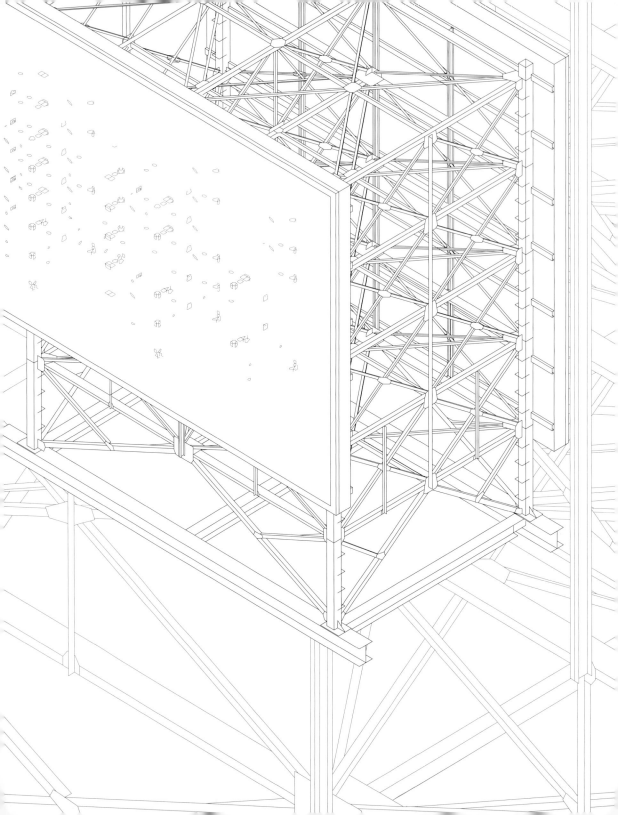

Practical Aspects of a Space of Invention
Kazuo Shinohara's House in Uehara

DAVID STEWART

Black & White Photographs © Koji Taki
Drawings © Shinohara Kazuo Estate/Titech, Tokyo

"Fictional space" was a term sometimes used by the late Kazuo Shinohara to characterize the architectural quality of his works. This could perhaps be better rendered in English as a "space of invention," and either translation is equally possible. The architect, who for many years dealt only in residential design, was forever on the lookout for something fresh and new. He did not pursue mere novelty of form, but rather sought to produce an experience of encounter in his houses with their multifarious spaces.

The miniscule House in Uehara (1976), whose name refers to a posh Tokyo district, inevitably also a crowded residential quarter, is a key work by this architect, who cultivated enigma but was at the same time the least enigmatic of beings. In this, it ranks with the celebrated House in White (Tokyo, 1966), the summerhouse for the poet Shuntaro Tanikawa (Karuizawa, 1974), and, finally, the architect's own modest but striking and original House in Yokohama (1985, now demolished).

Prior to his architectural training, Shinohara had studied mathematics and had a healthy respect for problem solving and the engineering aspects of buildings. Although many of his houses were at times considered bizarre accommodations to the client brief, that was partly owing to spatial constraints that led Shinohara, in many instances, to concentrate on a largish living (or reception) area as a "space" to the exclusion or relegation of more mundane areas of the residence. But this was a natural outcome of his early doctrine of the house as "art," or spatial encounter. It is also, possibly and in more generalized terms, a legacy of the traditional Japanese dwelling where rooms, to a certain extent, might be combined or subdivided to accommodate a change in use, function, or occasion. And, in fact, Shinohara was not the only Japanese architect to consider traditional Japanese construction as providing an essentially modular, layered, and frontal ambiance for various modes of human encounter, many humdrum or conventional to be sure but others of a more dramatic import. The fame and greatness of Japanese cinema may be seen to have paved the way for such conceptions, and modern Japanese

literature abets the notion of a space of encounter, its probabilities, and possible manifestations, particularly as considered, in retrospect, after 1945, if not actually up to and through the 1960s. Contemporary Japanese writing and the notorious "manga" culture, as it now flourishes both at home and abroad, might seem to prolong this existential quality but is actually parody of a rather gross sort. So, to be sure, is some contemporary architecture.

Indeed, iconic parody has a long tradition in the Japanese visual arts but hardly at all in those of building, with the exception of tea architecture. In the present instance, Shinohara once happened to compare the House in Uehara to the "savagery" implied in the title of the anthropologist Claude Lévi-Strauss's *Savage Mind* (1962). But that was an afterthought. And, in fact, on account of seismic codes, much Japanese work tends to be seen as over-dimensioned, hence, crude or overpowering, when such is not the case. Shinohara did point this out from time to time, and yet, at the same time, he was not exactly unhappy with the mildly outlandish dimensions of the enormous struts (almost "trees") that rise and proliferate in the structural resolution of the Uehara scheme.

How did this invention, itself fostering intimate encounter in a very constrained space, come about? In my own *Making of a Japanese Architecture* (1987) and elsewhere, most recently now in the posthumous volume of travel photographs taken by Shinohara and its accompanying album of selected works: *Street with Human Shadows* (Center for Contemporary Art, CCA Kitakyushu, 2006/2007) the explanation in practical terms is reiterated. Namely, the Uehara house conforms to a local height restriction but in such a way that it was able to include a 2.5-metre-width carport within the body of the structure, opening off the photographer's studio that occupies the adjacent ground floor enclosure. Finally, owing to the turning radius and to the narrowness of the lane in which the house stands there could be no support at the corner.

This trick of conserving vertical space was achieved by construction of a monolithic shell whose six upright pillars combine powerful diagonal struts poured parallel to the line of the main street façade. These elements are contained within the wall at front and back, but the two intermediate posts with their branch-like ramifications explode, so to speak, into the principal space of the dwelling, which is a "great room" of sorts, as Charles Moore would have called it. Here the space includes living, dining, and kitchen facilities, plus the mammoth and uncouth, if nonetheless beautiful, structural trees I have referred to.

All this was in order to permit a thin horizontal roof slab by channeling the bulk of the structure into the pillars and braces, eliminating the necessity for outsize beams in a horizontal dimension. As for the intermediate floor, this is not part of the reinforced-concrete structural scheme devised by the engineer Toshihiko Kimura and illustrated here in a contemporary blueprint drawing from his office. All flooring and wall partitions are of insulated lightweight inserted materials.

Apart from actual structural constraint and necessity, the shape of the concrete pillar units with their bracing derives in inspiration from the Tanikawa House referred to above, where similar post-and-strut units of squared timber supported the roof of an expansive two-story "summer" space, timber-framed and earth-floored, the house having been completed two years earlier. There the drama (or "fiction" or "invention," if one prefers to use one of these other

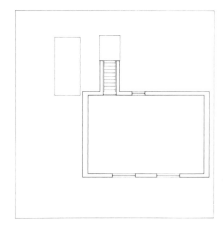

Third floor plan

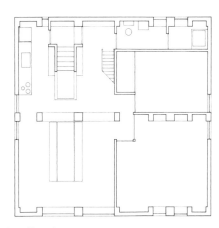

Second floor plan

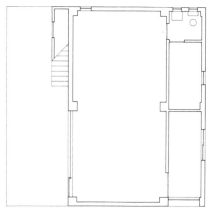

First floor plan

terms) lay in traversing a natural slope of exposed earth as part of a well-lit interior space (illustrated in both books cited above). Reverting to the earlier House in White, the conceit or invention there had originated in the architect's selection of a temple form (taken from a unique but well known historic Buddhist hall by the nearly legendary twelfth-century monk-builder Chogen, who oversaw the restoration of Todai Temple) to match, almost certainly for the first time in Japanese building history, the brief of an ordinary residence. Once more, then, in all three cases, the "house as art" and as an astonishing space of encounter!

Since the building history of the Japanese nation (and, here, one must *not* refer to an "architectural" tradition, in part because the notion of the architect and his calling is of such recent foundation) has been fraught with notions of decorum, all three examples culminating with Kazuo Shinohara's Uehara house were iconoclastic. Here I concentrate on Uehara, because one need not be Japanese, or a Japanese architect, to comprehend the newfound species of beauty at work beyond the perceived violence and fragmentation of this tiny interior. As will be evident from the original working drawings shown in the following pages, and especially those of the intermediate floor with its Great Room, the process — as always with Shinohara — entailed absorbing precision and economy of means.

This living space is the single event that is encapsulated, and indeed proliferates, in the dwelling. The downstairs office is a workspace, once more of substantial economy, while the uppermost floor, like the earlier mentioned application of the notion of "savagery," was an afterthought. The Quonset hut shaped protuberance set on the roof slab was designed as a much needed children's room, but in the form it took was able to be passed off serendipitously as a storage space, which, as such, was unaffected by the building code in force. And, serendipitously, too, it embodies and enhances the *bricolage* (do-it-yourself) quality of the whole, another term beloved of Lévi-Strauss. And, yet the Great Room with its great sculptured uprights is a mere by-product of, and thus integral to, the device of the structure that made possible the house that Shinohara built on what for almost any other designer would have been an all too restrictive site.

In this way, the space if not the house itself came, in what is a very tight fit, to express or stand for the very process that created it. This was one version of what Shinohara was fond of referring to as Symbolism, or symbolic space, where, in this case, the practical invention can, by reversal, read as a fictional one. Of all his works, then, this Fiction or this Invention at Uehara, is the most self-sufficient, evident, and concise. Like Nietzsche, Shinohara delighted in aphorism, a term that derives from the Greek verb translatable as "to define" from horos, a limit. A final thought, related to the architect's interest in mathematics, is that Shinohara was frankly intrigued by the topological properties of geometrical figures, those properties that remain unchanged even when the figure is manipulated by bending or stretching. Thus, as in the second-floor plan shown here, he often blew up details to a greater scale than the rest of the plan as a whole, a stretching that — while aiding the builder — left the relationships of the whole "unaffected" and uninfluenced. Not surprisingly, I believe, there is something of the po-faced spirit of the Austrian architect Adolf Loos here.

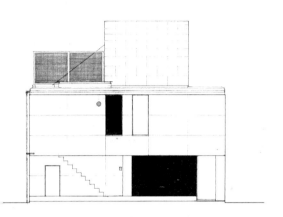

西 立面図

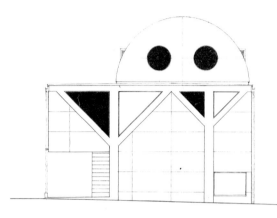

南 立面図

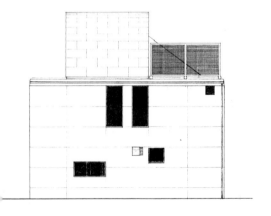

東 立面図

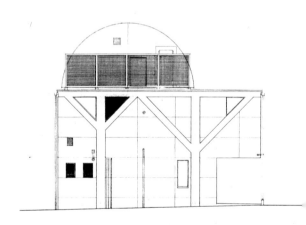

北 立面図

大社
訂正 51 08 2 1
SUBJECT
立面図

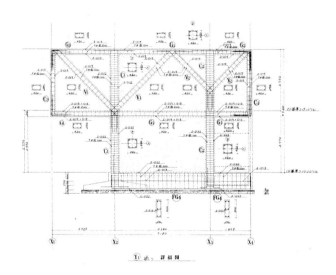

Y₁ 通り 詳細図

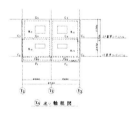

X₄ 通り 軸組図

S-3
木村俊彦構造設計事務所

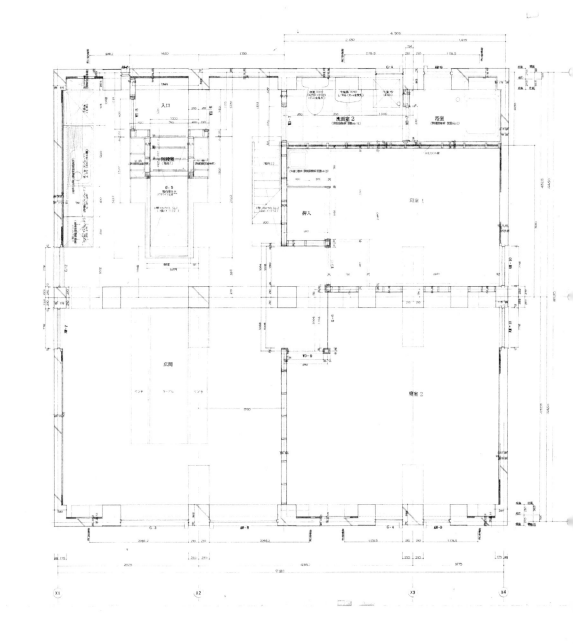

入口

入口

G-5

洗面室 2

浴室

押入

寝室 1

広間

寝室 2

訂正 51.09
research OB
大辻邸
date   scale 1:20
subject
2階 平面図
no. 03

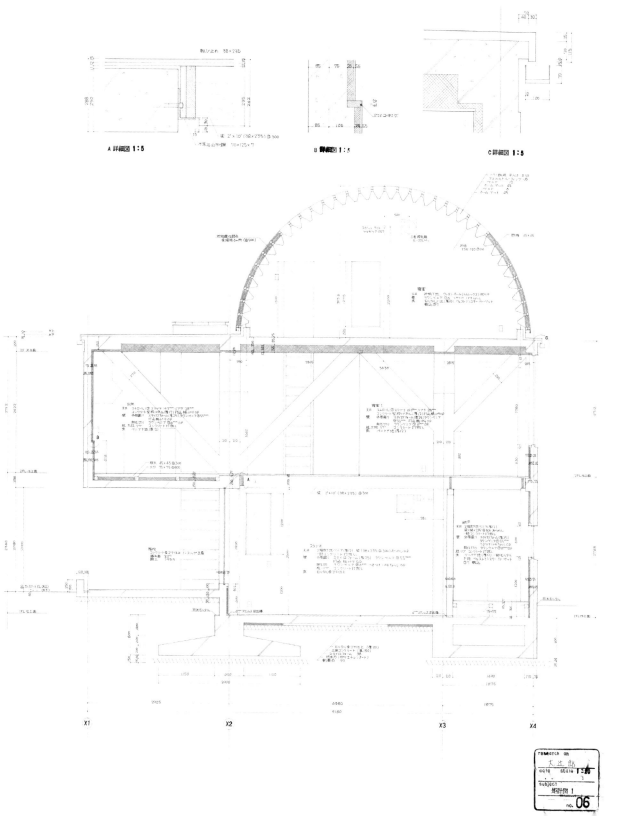

A 詳細図 1:5

B 詳細図 1:5

C 詳細図 1:5

X1   X2   X3   X4

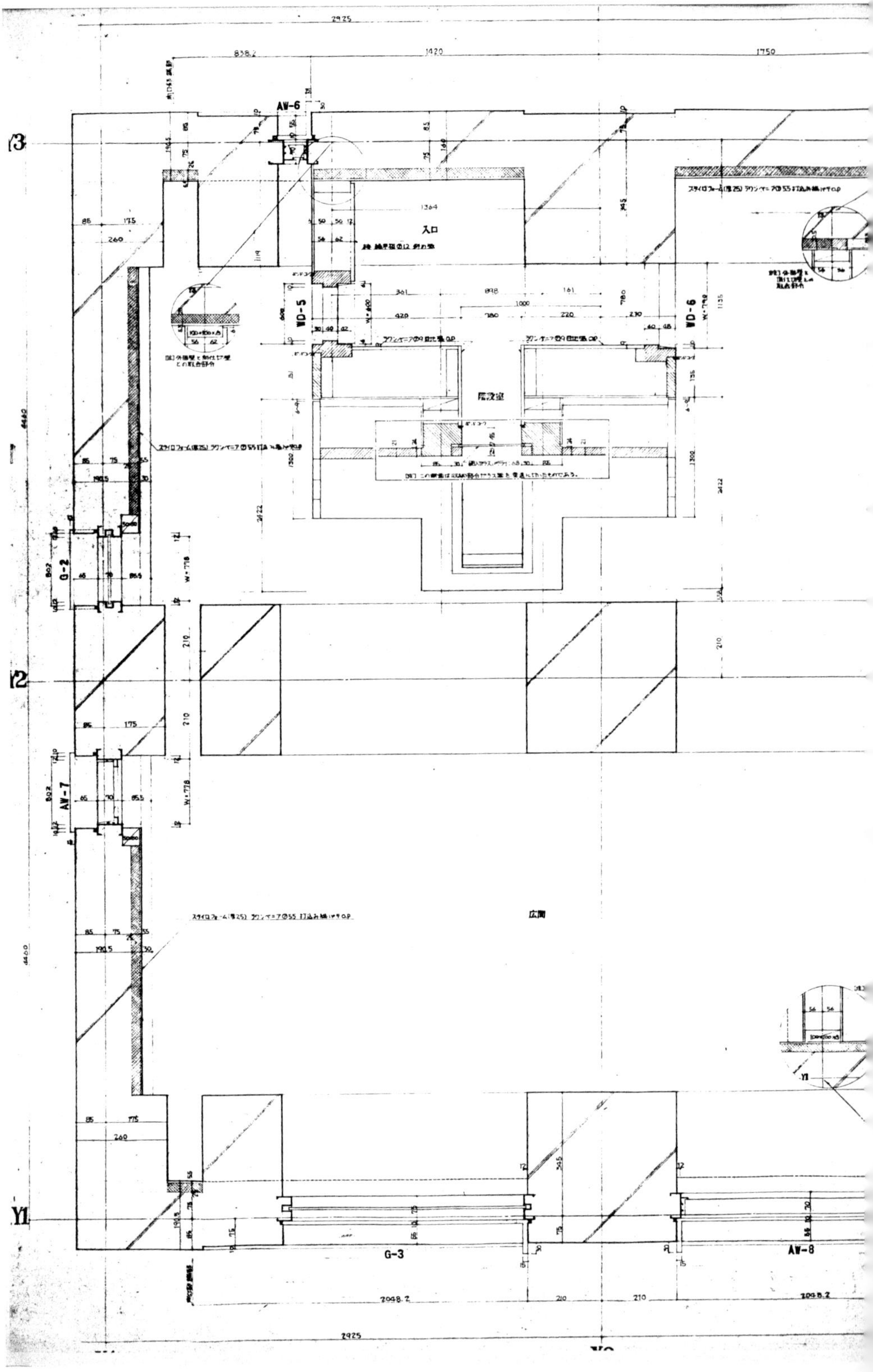

入口

広間

昇降路

AW-6
AW-7
AW-8
VD-5
VD-6
G-2
G-3

Y3
Y2
Y1

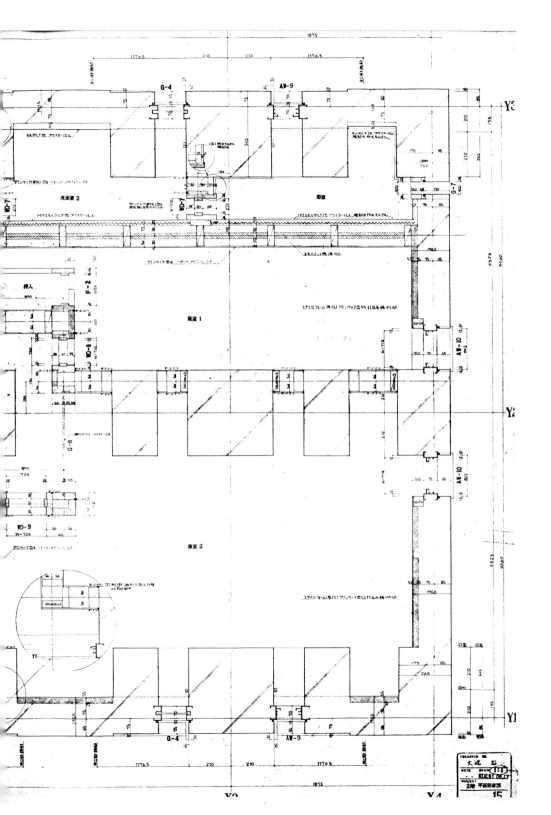

Shinohara Received

JOHN BASS

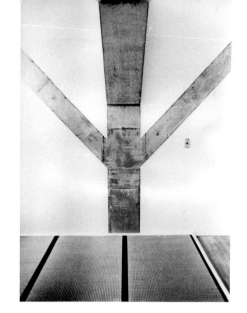

"Posts, walls, and braces express nothing but their own functions…I would like to eliminate, completely, if possible, various meanings derived from a spatial frame comprised of these elements." Kazuo Shinohara wrote this in the mid-nineteen seventies, a period when he was defining what he called his third style, one characterized by the production of "naked reality" and the elimination of overt symbolic reference. Describing his House in Uehara (1976) in *The Savage Machine as an Exercise*, Shinohara refers to the collection of diagonal elements in its second floor space — enormous lateral braces, stair enclosures, windows, and surface patterns — as a "jungle" and an example "savage space."[1] Shinohara then refers to Levi-Strauss's discussion in *The Savage Mind* of the paradoxical human desire to produce symbols despite their inevitable concretization. This paradox is at the core of what makes the second floor space of House in Uehara so powerful. It is a space that the body must navigate carefully, preferably equipped with a machete.

While reading Shinohara's essays one encounters a mind working incessantly to span theory and practice, a mind that respects and acknowledges both. His *Savage Machine* essay provides cover for the House in Uehara's cagily disinterested massing as well as the nearly intolerable tension between occupant, space, and occupying structure. Functionalism, Shinohara suggests, is simultaneously both indifferent to and the vessel of meaning. But it is not the functionalism of the 1920's. In his *Towards Architecture* (is the choice of title lost on anyone?) essay, published by the Institute for Architecture and Urban Studies in 1982,[2] he likens the streamlined biplane idealized by Le Corbusier to an "ornamental waterfowl afloat on a pond."[3] He then suggests that the new standard is a "clumsily connected" but state-of-the-art U.S. fighter jet design that "perform[s] its functions with maximum efficiency." He ends the essay by distancing himself from past functionalist rhetoric when he asserts "…my machine will not be international. It will have a name and nationality clearly indicated." Teaching and practicing in Tokyo, capital of the Empire of Signs, Shinohara declares his wish to erase all semantic traces from his work, and replace it with a compelling case for saying nothing — silence situated in a particular place and time in the world.

That Shinohara became a project for the IAUS is likely due to his synthesis of these two familiar but typically opposed arguments. Shinohara's interest in structuralist theory would certainly bring him to the attention of Peter Eisenman; and Shinohara's situated, tectonic modernism, to Kenneth Frampton. Shinohara's rejection of extreme formalism ("[t]hey placed operation on top of operation and pursued this simplistic one-way street to still further operations…")[4] would have made him an entertaining sparring partner for Eisenman. But it was with Frampton that sustained interaction occurred. His cultivation of Shinohara began with the 1982 IAUS catalogue, a year before Frampton's seminal essay "Towards a Critical Regionalism: Six Points for an

Architecture of Resistance" was published in *The Anti-Aesthetic*. 1983 was also the year that Yale journal *Perspecta* published an essay on Shinohara's ideas and works — and Frampton's essay "Prospects for a Critical Regionalism."

In 1984, Shinohara was the first to hold the Eero Saarinen Visiting Professorship of Architectural Design at Yale, the school where Patricia Patkau received her Master's degree in 1978. All of this activity centred on Shinohara would have exposed Patricia and her partner, John Patkau, to Shinohara's work. And while Shinohara was received on the east coast as a participant in an academic culture where the tie between theory and practice was growing tenuous, the Patkaus, just beginning to practice in British Columbia, saw something else in his House in Uehara. In Masao Arai's aqueous color photograph[5] of its "problematic" (as Shinohara called it) second floor space, the Patkaus saw idea and experience bound together. In this and other work of Shinohara, they saw abstract yet firmly situated buildings that acknowledged the mute poetics of site, structure, light, material, and body. For the Patkaus, and their own emerging theory of architecture, Shinohara's desire to wring meaning out of a "spatial frame" was not an argument about architecture's absolute *discursive* autonomy. Instead the Patkaus saw an argument about the immediacy of buildings and the critical role of material specificity — the only effective way to project intent onto a thing under one's control until, one day, it is released into the world.

[1] Kazuo Shinohara, "The Savage Machine as an Exercise," *The Japan Architect*, no. 7903, pp. 46-51. The reference to Levi-Strauss is on page 49.

[2] Kenneth Frampton and Silvia Kolbowski, editors. *Kazuo Shinohara*, Institute for Architecture and Urban Studies Catalogue 17, (Rizzoli, 1982). The 118-page catalogue was only the third English language text (of any type) not published in Japan that was devoted to exclusively to Shinohara's work. The first, creepily titled "Jap savagery," was published in *Architectural Review* in August 1977. Before the IAUS catalogue, the only other non-Japanese texts dedicated to Shinohara's work were in the Italian journal *Abitare* (1975, three pages on Shinohara's reinvention of tradition) and in the French *Architecture d'aujourd'hui*, which published his "Theory of Residential Architecture" essay in 1968. Both included English translations of the original Italian and French. Of course, Shinohara's buildings and ideas would have been accessible to English readers in the pages of *The Japan Architect*, and in articles surveying contemporary Japanese architecture, such as the Hajime Yatsuka essay in *Oppositions 23*.

[3] Ibid., 11

[4] Ibid., 13. The translation in the IAUS catalogue is a slightly different, tempered version of the one cited here, which is taken from Shinohara's "Towards Architecture" essay published in *The Japan Architect*, no. 8109, pg. 33.

[5] Ibid., 74

Speculations across Distance

Kazuo Shinohara's House in Uehara

PATRICIA PATKAU

There are always, for architects, buildings not yet visited but nevertheless influential in our minds. Publications makes access "of a sort" to a history and world of construction, an access with only the fragile hope for partial digestion. That digestion is enhanced and distorted by imaginary readings and misinterpretations rendered via partial documentation, photographs, and drawings. These projects establish their influence over the years, sticking in our minds like glue. Shinohara's work is such a work for this architect. It exists as a kind of irritant, so relentlessly unknown, so seemingly inexplicable at first impact. While a closer study of available, compiled material somewhat dispels the strangeness of this body of work, it does not eradicate the unease. The following is a speculation across distance on Shinohara's Uehara house in Tokyo, fueled only by incomplete publications and distorted readings. It is one way that we know what we know as architects.

In his writings, Shinohara positions his body of work culturally, firmly grounded in the context and spatial discourses of Japan, yet simultaneously fully engaged in those of a contemporary world. He tracks his own work, year by year, project by project, continuously reflecting on a personal and ongoing inquiry. While his work has undergone a series of transformations over his career, certain ideas persist. He says he wants to carve eternity in spaces, that he is interested in the non-rational, in making waste space, in draining space, material, and elements of their meaning. Formulating syntax to address such issues is obviously an ambitious and intriguing task. While he manages to clarify the intent of his work via his writings, only the works themselves can illuminate their syntactic resolution. Only the work itself can point to the facts of its direct and experienced impact.

In the House in Uehara (Tokyo, 1976), a clear syntactic question posed by the work is one of time: what came first? There is a definite and immediate sense of sequence imparted in both time and construction. The material presence and figuration of the columns can only be considered as totemic, as primary and as "first." They have "been" before space was incidentally accrued around them. They are in no way inclined to accommodate inhabitation in the spaces they construct. They in no way acknowledge daily life. They are just "as is." A force. Inexplicable. Immutable and ineffable presences. These columns are an occupational force, their symmetry and outstretched arms strangely relate to the body's while in no way acknowledging the bodies of others. They are figures that people have to negotiate around carefully so as not to hurt themselves. In spite of their extended arms, the columns do not act dynamically in space so much as merely existing there. These timeless figurations are a form of syntactic exploration, attempting to void form of rational associations. They are structural support but we don't read this as their primary reference. They construct space, but they don't seem interested in this act. We are alternately attracted and repulsed by their status as non-organic beings. In Shinohara's work this primary figuration of the column with its outstretched arms is used over and over again, to occupy rather than to construct space. Human beings are relegated to an incidental secondary role. The braced columns impart a sense of time and endurance in the face of the domestic and daily.

Shinohara talks about the difference in spatial ideas of time between the West and Japan. In reference to Japanese spatial devices he suggests that "… compositions characterized by spatial division are normally static, in that the movement of people through them is rarely taken into consideration," and that "This unique concept contrasts sharply with the Western approach, which, since the days of ancient Greece, has traditionally been to build courtyards or connective spaces leading to various compartments. The existence of spaces where people walk about has introduced the concept of time into Western architecture. This, generally speaking, is the basis of the dynamic concept of Western space." (114) He continues in another vein: "In Japanese art, the protagonist's role is static, with dynamism relegated to a supporting role. But this immobility does not in any way imply lifelessness. It is instead — as the dramatic value of immobility in Noh theater illustrates — a condensation of time and life." In Japan then space is static and divided without a referential space for movement. Movement is anywhere, everywhere, incidental to spatial organization. In this static field condition, the static is dramatic, a dense essence of time and life. Movement is implied, both a ghost like memory of drifting figures and a constant possibility of new appearances. Relating this cultural interpretation of space to the Uehara house, the columns, the "most static" elements, are dramatically charging the spaces around them with their immobility. And, if as Shinohara suggests, immobility is imbued with a condensation of time and life, then the protagonists in the Uehara house, the braced columns, are both a kind of charged immobility and almost human — enduring and timeless bodies.

If we turn our attention to the relationship between column, brace, and space, we are somewhat confounded. The regularity in plan of the two central spaces, (almost squares at 4380mm x 4325mm), with their attendant columns at each corner, would imply in rational terms that the columns have equal arm lengths in the centre bay (diagram) each carrying half the load. This is not the case. And, as the design for the first two levels was completed before the owner decided to add the third floor, this inequity in loading does not seem to be due to structural loads received from the third floor. We could understand irregular spans occurring in the edge bays (due to the difference in length of spans and loading) but irregularity in span makes little sense in the central bays. By being unequal in length and springing from different heights above the floor, the braces belong to one column only. We can't read columns and braces as a system of support. We are forced to associate arms and columns in sets as figures. A rational and normative reading of structure is consciously denied. We are left then with the non-rational or the rational deployed to other ends. There is a constant syntactic effort here to disrupt expectation, to deny apparent logics in architecture, to suggest that this is somehow "other," not yet known, perhaps even incapable of being understood by reason alone.

The deployment of all secondary elements such as walls, counters, and stairs reinforces a sense of the temporariness of human occupation in the face of the

primary and enduring columnar occupation. Kitchen counters and appliances seem to be an afterthought, pushed up against a wall with the above counter exhaust fan and side of the oven presenting a dismal elevation to the living and dining areas. The necessities of daily living have no resolution in terms of their depth and positioning. They do not participate in constructing space. If people feel the need of such things in their daily life, they will just have to find a place for them somewhere. They are not part of any syntax for the building. There is little evidence of a concern for human comfort or for the daily aspects of dwelling in this architecture.

Two diagonals, the entrance stair enclosure and the diagonal in the opposite direction, the interior stair to the third floor, produce a tension that is other than the tension of the occupying force of columns. These diagonal forces are active slashes in space which promise an accommodation for the human body as it negotiates the section. Witnessing this accommodation, the columns are rendered even more passive and disinterested. Stairs cannot avoid a reference to our own scale and bodily dimensions while the columns need not pander to us in any way; they are simply oblivious to such concerns. The entrance door to the second floor confirms indifference, its pentagonal form derived from the underside of an overhead brace.

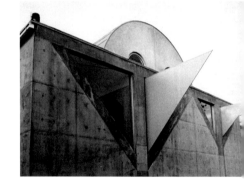

The Uehara house has an extreme interiority which isolates the spaces of the living and dining level in time and circumstance. The sense is of an internalized, somewhat strange world, one that is of its own making. Relief comes when the giant shutters open ninety degrees but the sense of strangeness remains in the triangular acquired views. When open, the sharply pointed shutters are aggressive, defensive of interior space. Both the triangular windows and air shutters are merely left over spaces between braces and columns, the void spaces of the columns. They are formed through this relationship, not from any relationship to occupation or to any consideration of site. Interiority is only really distracted by the captured glance of someone approaching from below (seen via the slanted window overlooking the main entrance stair). Odd reflections from the sloped glazing over the entrance distort and collapse inside and outside, projecting abnormal relationships of surveillance and anticipation into a private realm.

Shinohara says of the Uehara house that "The large spaces that I have always been preoccupied with are absent here, replaced by a collection of small spaces that gave rise to the newly problematic concept of savagery." Elsewhere in his descriptions of his own work, he does not suggest that conceptual intent or consequence is "problematic." In a later house, his 1978 House on a Curved Road in Tokyo, he acknowledges an interest in expressing unity through this same notion of savagery. In this house there is an equally vigorous structural expression but, perhaps due to the larger volumes — volumes that allow the robust column braces to exist well above head height — the savagery is not considered problematic? Here savagery, if it really exists, is tamed and controlled in relationship to the human body. Here the savagery is an experience of the columnar elements in space not an aggressive act of the column towards the body in restricted space. This taming may be why the word "problematic" does not occur in a description of the Curved Road House. It is savagery that is different in kind. Yet both do achieve a kind of unity through another idea, the "idea of man-made nature" (31), a compelling timeless rawness, a force that gathers space to it. This man-made nature is steeped in our ambivalence towards it. We are caught, oscillating between attraction and repulsion, like metal filings in a magnetic field.

How is it that a culture can support a body of work that is so far from solicitous, so far from any norms in its considerations of dwelling? Shinohara argued that "from the start I sought to base my work on the traditions of Japanese architecture and to this end argued against rationalism and functionalism, which were the main forces in the architectural world at the time." (26) His is a unique vision, a culturally specific act capable of forcefully engaging a located human psyche and physiology. While projected from the Japanese cultural landscape, the work's direct material impact empathetically resonates across cultural divides. Amidst current inclinations in architectural discourse that again preface rationalism as sufficient process and programmatic interpretation as sufficient argument, Shinohara insists that it might be possible to carve eternity into space. He links mind, sensation, and matter suggesting both our significance as fully sensate, intuitive, and complex beings and our insignificance in a universe of time.

"I tried to search for time within the spaces of Japanese architecture. It was an impossible undertaking. All I found was expanse without time." (114)

Kenneth Frampton and Silvia Kolbowski, editors. *Kazuo Shinohara*, Institute for Architecture and Urban Studies Catalogue 17, (Rizzoli, 1982).

House in Uehara – Kazuo Shinohara

JOHN PATKAU

I look at photographs and drawings of the house in Uehara from a distance. By this I do not mean, simply, that I am not close to the house, that I have not visited the house recently — I have not visited the house at all. By this I mean that I look at the photographs and drawings of the house in Uehara without explanation. I look at these images of the house without knowing the architect's intentions, without understanding the culture within which it has been constructed. This is sufficient for me; the house (and not even the house itself, just photographs and drawings of the house) is all I need, and want.

I am overwhelmed by the presence of the thing, especially the archaic presence of the raw concrete figures that occupy the space. Within the domain of these eternal objects, life is provisional. The kitchen is simply a collection of equipment temporarily set-up in the corner of the space, the stair to the attic only a ladder. Life goes on in this space, but it is transitory. The house is at once a humbling expression of the frailty of human life, and at the same time a triumphant claim for the power of architecture. It is a declaration by the architect, on behalf of us all, that the mind, and the imagination, can outlive the body, can aspire to immortality.

Is there more to say? Not much. There is the specific story of the owner, the owner's needs and wants; the architect and his ambitions; the site and its geographic and cultural context. These things are interesting and informative — the addition of the vaulted space on the roof certainly adds to, or diminishes, or at least changes the architect's original intentions, but it does not alter the fundamental force of the structure. It is another provisional piece of equipment, a tent mounted on the roof to make the house accommodate the needs of the initial inhabitant. It can stay or it can go, it does not matter.

Perhaps the ambition for an eternal architecture is naïve. We all know that nothing is forever. We know that a time will come when we no longer exist, when the sun and the earth will no longer exist, when even time will no longer exist. This, also, does not matter. What matters to us is our existence, our time, our sun and earth.

The house in Uehara is the work of a mature mind; the work of a long life, lived. It is the work of a mind contemplating death. Not all architecture can do this; most architecture should not even attempt to do this. It is a special case, the product of a special sensibility, a sensibility that took a lifetime to evolve. The house in Uehara is the last word. For me, it is Shinohara's last word, even though I know that chronologically it is not Shinohara's last work. After this, nothing further needs to be said.

BIKE PARK (04)

The use of bicycles as a common method of travel in Tokyo has yielded an array of bicycle parking structures, far more advanced than the structures typically found in North America. Available in a multitude of configurations, all bicycle racks seek to maximize parking density by staggering stalls, preventing neighbouring handlebars from bumping into one another. Vast stretches of parking racks can be found sheltered near train stations, forming an urban spatial experience unique to Tokyo.

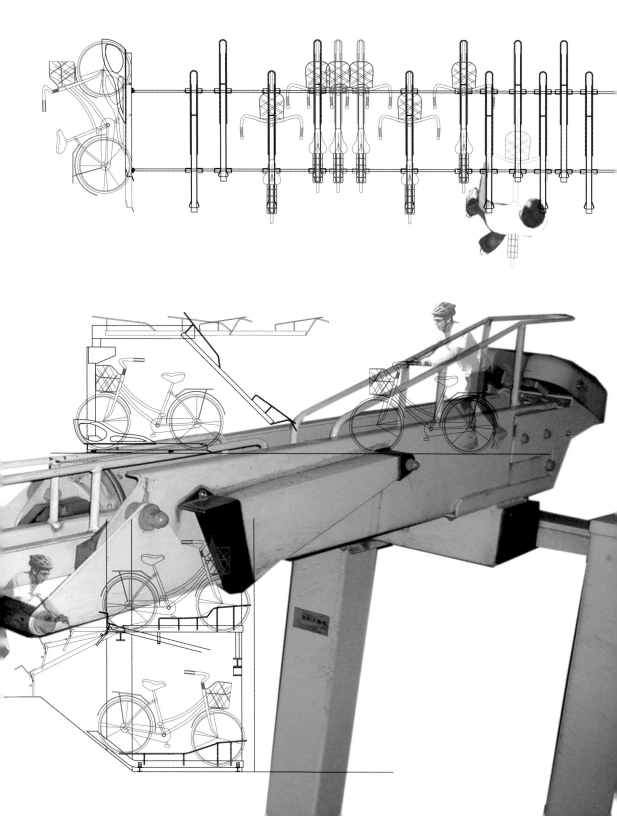

Platform (Tokyo, 2006)
View from Eda Station

Courtyard

Platform

MANABU CHIBA

Platform is a collective housing project of rental units for 62 households located in front of a railway station in suburban Tokyo. By virtue of the site's existence amongst a dense urban infrastructure, consisting of a station-front plaza, railway tracks, an expressway and a national highway, we interpreted its surroundings as a large spatial void. From the particularity of the context came the concept for the structure itself: an urban scaled building set amidst a large empty space.

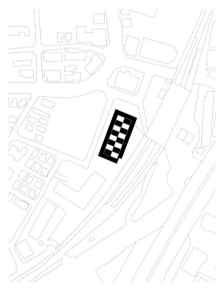

Site plan, 1:4000

View toward station

2nd floor plan

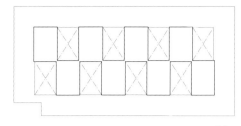

roof plan

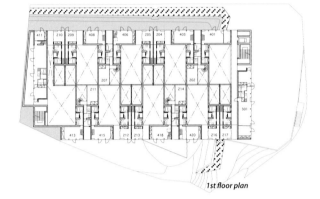

1st floor plan

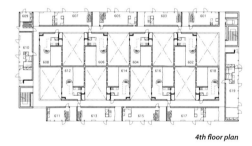

5th floor plan

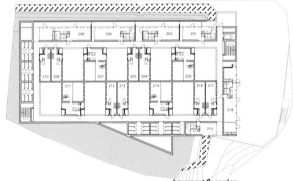

basement floor plan

4th floor plan

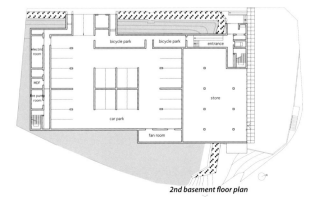

3rd floor plan

2nd basement floor plan

The building was therefore conceived as a mass that has both a clear spatial structure and is of a varied spatial character. This understanding coincides with our notion of the structure of cities. The structure aspires to the dynamic condition of residing in the city by reconciling the need for both neighbourly contact and private living.

Balcony overlooking station

The building's structure is straightforward, consisting of two types of spaces, paralleling the twofold organization of the common Japanese city block. The first type, the perimeter, consists of a horizontal band that constitutes the 'outer shell' of the site. Measuring 3.6m in depth, it orients itself towards the surrounding void space, while simultaneously wrapping the interior to protect it from noise. The other is a vertical space that marks the center of the structure, consisting of a checkerboard pattern of two-story units. It is characterized as quiet and inward looking. The 62 units that constitute Platform are thus the combinative result of these two spaces created in relationship with the outside world. Throughout the building, both 'shell' and center are freely combined, creating a series of interlocked spaces resembling a three-dimensional puzzle. The design therefore distances itself from the repetition of identical units that is common for larger scale residential developments.

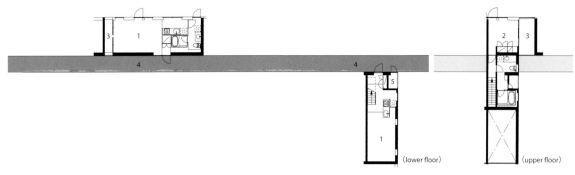

A type

B type

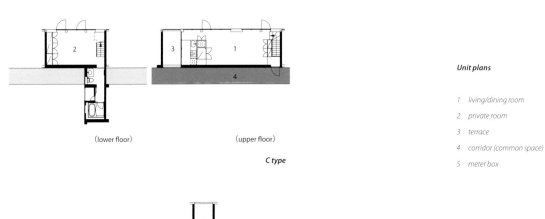

(lower floor)

(upper floor)

C type

Unit plans

1 living/dining room

2 private room

3 terrace

4 corridor (common space)

5 meter box

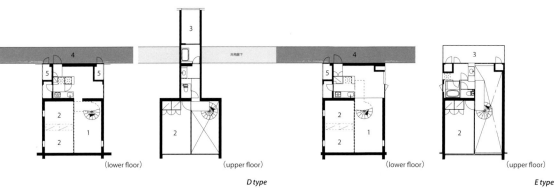

(lower floor)

(upper floor)

D type

(lower floor)

(upper floor)

E type

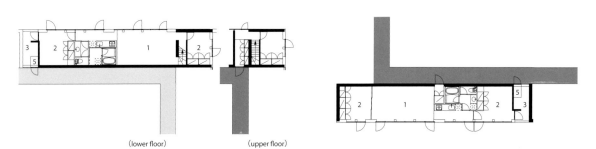

(lower floor)

(upper floor)

F type

G type

B type unit, kitchen and living

Because the size of the housing complex was almost large enough to be a small town, an early working premise was that the building ought to be an assembly of varied units. To promote variety, all units intertwine and interrelate with one another as though vying for position. Each unit's space will at times expand in an unexpected direction, with its own unique configuration of horizontal and vertical spaces. Every unit has views in multiple directions suggesting an infinitely expanding space. Visual relationships within the building and out towards the surrounding environment abound. The experience of the building can be likened to walking through a small city where urban events occur spontaneously and disappear just as quickly.

E type unit, living room

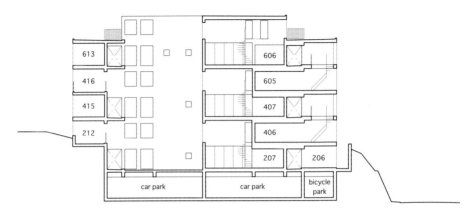

613			606	
416			605	
415			407	
212			406	
			207	206
car park		car park		bicycle park

Cross section, 1:400

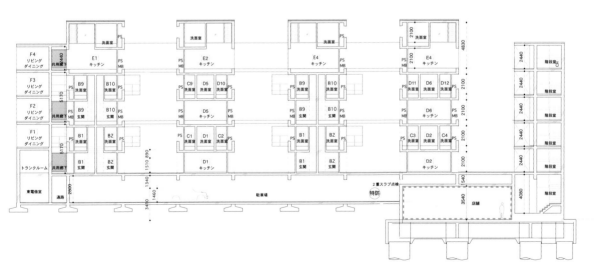

Long section, 1:400

Exterior circulation

Such a relationship where one is securely protected yet connected with the outside or one's own space is secured but connected to others is a fundamental joy of urban living. The project can also be seen as an attempt to create a microcosm of the city.

I believe that the larger the scale of housing complex, the greater the need for these spatial and sensory qualities. Although the organizing principle emerged from a strictly individual condition, once the project was completed, it began to look so natural as to suggest this had to be the prototype of all housing complexes. I believe that a structure possessing such potential may indeed become the platform to support life with utmost flexibility.

Unit balcony overlooking courtyard

ROADSIDE GARDENS

At the interface between street and sidewalk, the gardener utilizes existing curbs, sidewalks and road barriers as the site for an improvised garden comprising various sizes of square and rectangular planters, plastic crates and wooden shelves. Rebar and wire hold the garden together.

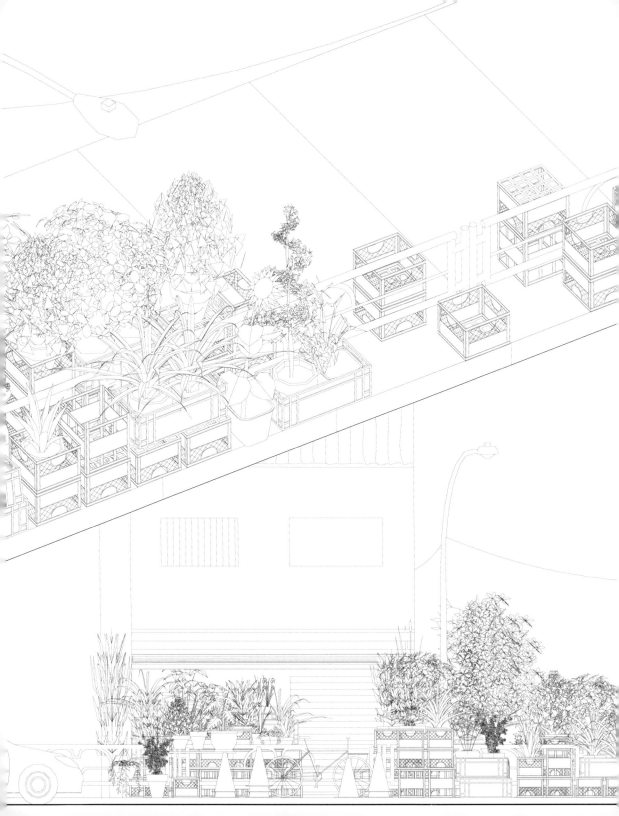

Build

DANA BUNTROCK

In Japan, two architects (both born in 1941) are often seen as the dynamic poles of practice. Osaka-born Tadao Ando is known for his refusal to theorize, deeply exploring a single-minded commitment to a relatively modest material, concrete. Tokyo-based Toyo Ito, a few months Ando's senior, is considered more deeply intellectual, observantly articulating the implications of social change. In the 1970s, Ito reflected the technological enthusiasm of the nation, originally calling his firm URBOT, an abbreviation of "Urban Robot." His work of this period ultimately culminated in "Silver Hut," a high-tech aluminum home for his family, where windows were cranked shut by the kind of mechanisms found in automobiles of the time and people sat on airy, expanded-metal chairs. The following year, 1985, Ito shifted gears, his investigations inaugurated by the first "Pao," a tent for "the Nomadic Woman of Tokyo," which suggested that many of the functions of the home were now diffused into the city's convenience stores, coin laundries, and social sites. This modest installation initiated a series of projects reflecting Ito's sense that society had become increasingly rootless, buildings ephemeral, and the reliable context for works little more than the wind; Ito's 1995 competition design for Sendai Mediatheque was the climax of this phase in his work. The program requirements for Mediatheque were ambiguous; in response, Ito offered up a technological playground for an urbane population, articulating the building as an open container that could be freely transformed over time. Initial variations in floor heights, finishes and lighting meant that no transformation would ultimately affect the building as a whole.

I was privileged to spend a great deal of time on the Mediatheque construction site, and I vividly recall Ito's struggles to come to terms with this building. The competition-winning model offered up a delicate filigree of lattice-like tubes supporting insubstantial floors, a sparkling, transparent

web; the actual structure on site was made of powerful pipes which seemed all the heavier because of their charcoal grey primer paints. Ito spoke often of his desire to erase this robust steel; vertical tubes were painted white and walls were finished in shimmering opalescent mirrors, but the strength of this remarkable structure could not be denied.

The exhibition "Toyo Ito: the New Real," held at Tokyo Opera City Art Gallery, opens with Ito's recollections of this crucial moment in his practice. While Ito's voice is not a significant part of the exhibition, in the opening text panel in the first gallery he speaks directly: "Visiting the Sendai Mediatheque construction site, I was overwhelmed by the power of the tremendous steel structure. The crane danced steel panels through the air, sparks fluttered around me, and the acrid scent of welding filled the air. This was entirely different than the usual construction site.... Could I turn towards a richer architecture, of deeper materiality? After Sendai, I began to grope for a solution." (Translated from the original by this author. Most of the panels and labels in the galleries are solely in Japanese; the catalogue includes English translations of critical texts.)

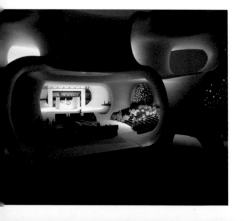

Oddly, the work highlighted in this room is not Mediatheque, and in fact is a project that seems almost antithetical to Ito's statement. The gallery features the competition-winning designs for a single, unbuilt project, the December 2005 proposal for the Taichung (Taiwan) Metropolitan Opera House. A huge model, 1.8 metres wide by 3.8 metres long and a metre tall, sits on an even larger base; a park-like space in front of the opera house is represented by a second, 8.4-metre-long model that fills the room. These models present the building's fluidly labyrinthine interiors as an extension of the natural world, a honeycomb of hourglass-like volumes accommodating a cave-like continuous flow of public spaces and barely-enclosed theatres for the performing arts, unlike any completed building that one has ever seen. Panels along one

wall argue for the care taken in assuring that this project is as buildable as it is unbelievable; computer simulations show how the open halls will perform acoustically and how structural forces are distributed along the shell-like skin, while technical drawings offer up two plausible construction approaches that can be employed to create these curvaceous interiors. The room that follows immediately reinforces this argument, filled with a full-scale mock-up of the sinuous formwork for the recently completed Crematorium in Kakamigahara (in Gifu Prefecture, Japan). The mockup is stained and clearly built from the materials used at the time of construction. Gallery visitors timidly climb on this rolling surface, unaware of the experience to come as they pass across the steep, undulating floor of the next space.

It is this third room that is the heart of the exhibition, reflecting Ito's current excitement with structural innovation. Six large models are salted across a landscape-like floor built for the exhibition, the long walls of the space covered with six-metre-tall construction documents — sections, at full scale. Five small video screens show each project from sketch through construction through inhabitation for completed buildings like Tods, Mikimoto Ginza 2, and the Serpentine Pavilion, or concentrate on the remarkable construction process of works as yet incomplete; some of the construction documents and photographs from this room are also found in the catalogue to the exhibition. A portion of the web-like facade of the 2004 Tods Omotesando materializes along the narrow wall opposite the entry, abstract drawings on the left blending seamlessly with cabinet-quality formwork, the interstices filled with rebar at the mid-point of the wall, and a "completed" section to the right, apparently concrete, but in fact simply a very convincing application of mortar over wood.

While architects and construction professionals can only be transfixed by the rich content of the videos and drawings — explaining ground-breaking

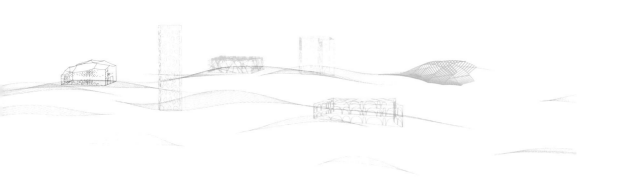

construction innovations in wood, steel, and concrete — for the public, the room's fascination lies quite literally in its topographical floor. The white surface contorts like a landscape of snowdrifts into which some active group of children has carved pits adjacent to each architectural model, the better to peer into their interiors. The playful character of these hollows is underscored by their pastel colors, which contrast with the otherwise modernist palette of the space. (Drawings on the walls are black lines on white, and the models are mostly charcoal grey, with the occasional introduction of an actual material such as mortar or wood.) People you would not expect to find in an architectural exhibition, bent grandmothers and small children, giggle, climb down into the pits, and linger. The space collects groups in conversation, seemingly unaware of how Ito has again created an architecture, albeit a temporary installation, that effectively encourages social discourse. Although Opera City Gallery offers four shows a year, this is only the third architectural exhibition served up in these galleries (Yoshio Taniguchi was featured in 2005 and Jean Nouvel in 2003). Another followed in Spring, 2007, featuring the work Terunobu Fujimori brought to the 2006 Venice Biennale. Unlike the two earlier shows, this is a more lavish production, the first here to offer up the experience of being in works by the architect. Because of the costs involved, most architectural exhibitions rely on photographs and models, with perhaps smaller fragments of building. Ito has always tried to use installations to embrace the body and express the experience of his work, a practice that only a few other architectural designers (including Fujimori) have adopted. Without writing a word, Ito argues through this undulating floor and its effect that his work today, in spite of its fascination with innovative structure, remains one committed to community.

Beyond the mock-up of the Tods facade is an area that the Opera City Art Gallery conventionally uses for projecting videos. Here, visitors to the show will finally find a surprisingly modest display of materials related to Sendai Mediatheque, the project which first challenged Ito to take on his current quest. In order to display projections, the room is dimly lit; two panels and two tiny photographs (by the esteemed photographer Naoya Hatakeyama) are so discretely displayed on the walls flanking these projections that many may miss them. In a far corner, a glimmering model portrays that initial, ephemeral vision

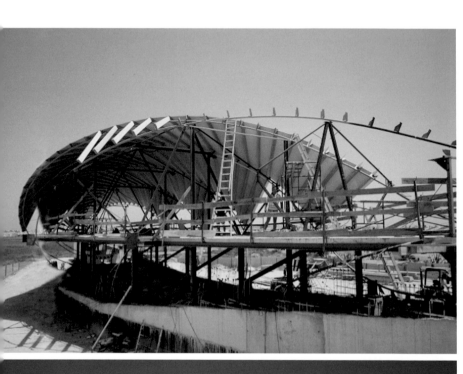

Ito hoped to achieve in Mediatheque.

As if to acknowledge this turning point, the exhibition shifts abruptly in the final, corridor-like space, where a 30-metre-long wall offers up a chronology of Ito's work from 1970 to the present. There is a remarkable level of extraneous but interesting detail here: a snapshot shows a young Ito in a flirtatious moment during a trip through the United States; noted under each year is the number of staff in the office (3 from 1971 all the way until 1977, still only a dozen in 1988, and 48 today); a video shows Kazuyo Sejima at the time she entered Ito's firm; and manuscript sheets for published texts show Ito's carefully rendered *kanji* characters neatly marching across the planes of gridded Japanese writing paper. Many of these materials are, thankfully, extensively documented in the accompanying catalogue, *Toyo Ito: The New "Real" in Architecture*. The chronology makes up almost one quarter of the book, followed by warm reminiscences by staff, excerpted from the videos (both sections only in Japanese). These charming additions serve to distract, however, from a rather subversive feature of this chronology: it is a gentle but deliberate revision of Ito's output, emphasizing the technological and spatially fluid. Missing are his digital infatuations and conception of two simultaneous modes of existence, expressed at installations at the Victoria and Albert Museum in 1991 and the 1993 exhibition at O Museum in Tokyo's Osaki, entitled "Digital Membrane, Buildings of Water," or his series of proposals for developing a rooftop network of gardens overlaying gritty Tokyo, starting with a series of "simulated cities" in the early 1990s. Ito's recent explorations of aluminum, including his 2005 SUS Company Housing in Fukushima and his 2006 aluminum cottage, are portrayed, but their minimal inclusion here certainly raises questions as to why these equally innovative buildings were not highlighted earlier in the exhibition.

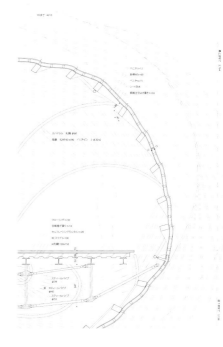

In discovering all the words on this wall, the stream of conversations on videos, the manuscripts, and the trade journals featuring Ito's work, one is struck by the fact that the theoretical ideas behind his current approach to architecture are unstated elsewhere. Instead, the show focuses on the formal nature of his buildings today, the manner in which these unusual structures emerge from a loosening of the Modernist grid and the new technological approaches he has squeezed from the conventional materials of construction.

As Opera City also has no internal curators, Ito and his office, working with the "Toyo Ito Exhibition Executive Committee," designed the exhibition and published the related catalogue themselves; this re-interpretation of Ito's work comes from the office.

Following an oddly placed set of non-architectural pieces (featuring the Ripple bench, scattered throughout the gallery, and frog-encrusted dishware for Alessi), the show culminates in a wall of hardhats, each marked with the name of a sponsor. The Tokyo Opera City Art gallery is part of a large cultural foundation established in 1999 that receives a modest $5-million annually from the Japanese government, with remaining costs covered through donations. Corporate supporters such as NTT Urban Development and Nippon Life Insurance offer on-going funding for operating costs and generous support for individual cultural events such as this show. In addition, the Ito office drew in forty-four other corporate sponsors for the exhibition: all five major contractors in Japan, an aluminum fabricator Ito has been working with for some time, major glass suppliers, Autodesk, and a variety of other corporations directly tied to the work on the wall. In spite of the generous corporate support, the closing helmets and discrete logos on entry tickets are the only place where the fabricators, suppliers, structural engineers, and contractors who help make Ito's work a reality are named — there are no labels attached to individual projects supplying data such as the construction team or building costs.

An earlier version of the undulating floor at the heart of this show was installed in Mies van der Rohe's Neue Nationalgalerie in Berlin in mid-2006. In the opening panel I mentioned earlier, and in the catalogue accompanying *The New 'Real' in Architecture*, Ito and others discuss his, and modern architecture's, debt to Mies. Ito counters the dry uniformity of Mies' grids with his loose, "emerging grid" and challenges Mies' famous aphorism "Less is More." But this show suggests another, unstated dictum credited to Mies, which Ito has embraced: "Don't talk, build." Through these varied and dynamic works, Ito challenges others to celebrate not merely the intellectual conception of their own architecture, but also to discover how deeper reflections on social and technological change may point to a new architecture, markedly different from the structures we know today.

Berlin – Tokyo Exhibition Photos © Christian Gahl

Opera City Exhibition Photos © Nacasa and Partners

Relaxation Park, Torrevieja, Alicante, Spain, Construction Photos © Oriol Rig

Tokyo Opera City Gallery, Tokyo, Japan. *Toyo Ito: the New "Real" in Architecture.*

Exhibition schedule: Tokyo Opera City Gallery, Tokyo, Japan, 7 October – 24 December, 2006; Sendai Mediatheque, Sendai, Japan, 13 April – 19 May, 2007; The Museum of Modern Art, Hayama, Japan, 9 June – 2 September, 2007. The show is expected to be offered at the University of California, Berkeley in 2008, probably in a modified form.

Discussions of the organization of the exhibition below are specific to its Tokyo setting. Information regarding this venue can be seen at: http://www.operacity.jp/ag/exh77/index_e.html

Toyo Ito: The New "Real" in Architecture. Tokyo: Toyo Ito Exhibition Executive Committee, 2006. 184 pp. 77 color ills.; 213 b/w. (3000 yen) (cloth) (4-925204-20-3 C0052).

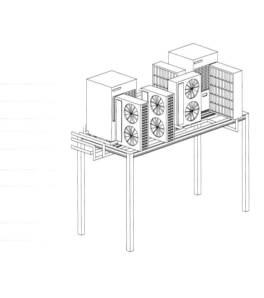

PARASITIC AIR

Reliance upon mechanical systems in Tokyo is emphasized by the accumulation of individual air conditioning units that exist in an ad-hoc manner, attaching themselves to buildings in parasitic ways. Through this accumulation the units achieve a new magnitude and ultimately a new form, creating an alternative relationship between building occupants and the machines that serve them.

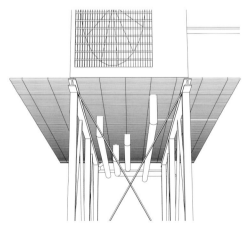

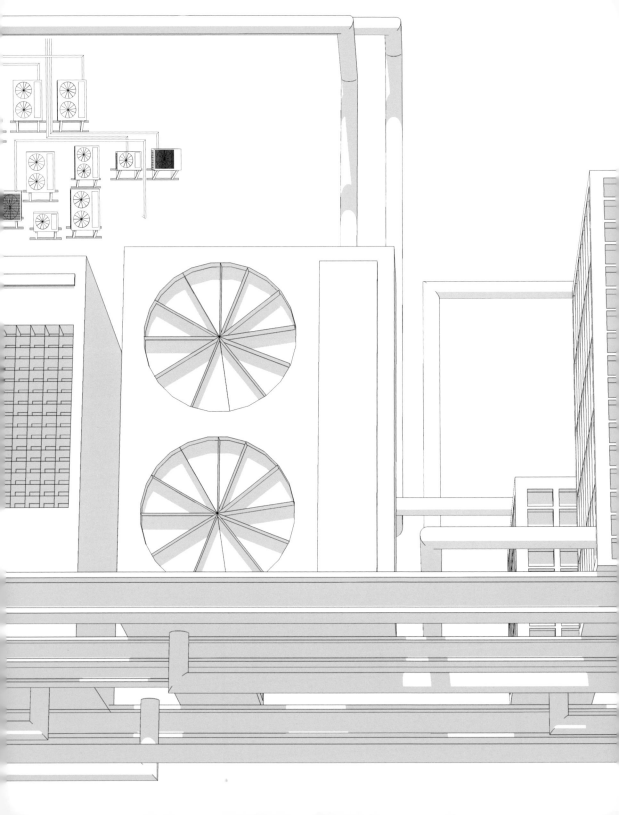

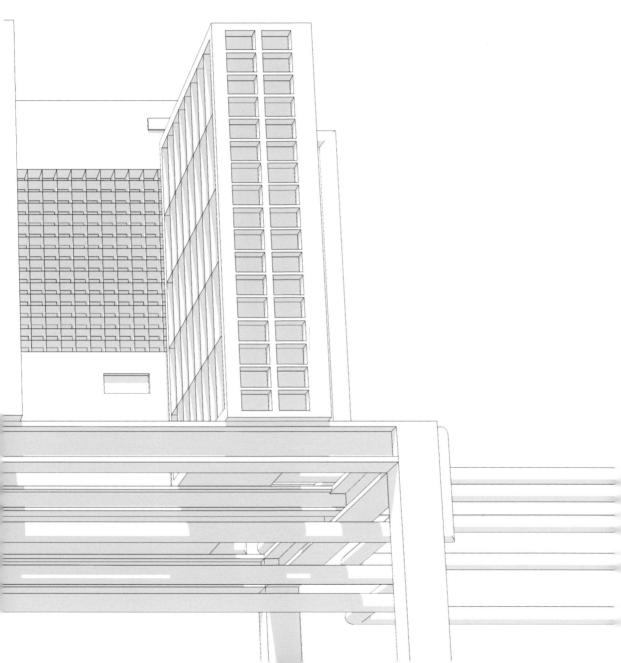

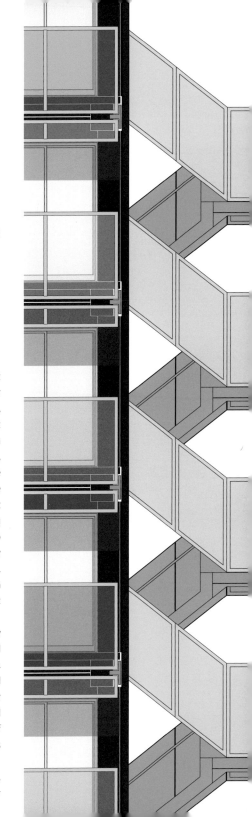

Diversity through Mass-Production
Two Examples of Mass Housing

YASUTAKA YOSHIMURA

Every year more than a million houses are built in Japan, and of those about 20 percent are prefabricated. It's a matter of opinion whether that number seems big or small. I recall that in 1963, the year before the Tokyo Olympics, 90 percent of new houses were traditional Japanese wooden structures built by local construction firms. That number certainly shows the structural shift in housing production. Not only statistically, but also from a consumer standpoint, it would not be an exaggeration to say that prefabricated houses are now the norm in Japanese housing production. I should mention, though, that the reality of the prefab industry in Japan is quite different from what Metabolist architects once assumed. Mass production's initial purpose of supplying housing at a low price and providing a large free floor space soon shifted to securing a certain degree of diversity. From the beginning, there was clearly a demand for quality that was not being satisfied by existing house builders. Mass production houses persisted with the pitched roof type, even though the angle is much sharper than necessary for water protection — a symbolic meaning was given to it. This situation has not changed.

Although I mentioned "a certain degree of diversity," it is clear that diversity is not essential. The house builder's brochure is as colorful as the seasonal catalogs for furniture and cars: the impression is that they all look the same. In fact, housing cannot be changed drastically, even if the assembly method is somewhat different, because it relies on third parties, such as the sash or water equipment manufacturer. People interested in prefab houses demand "suburban," "European," and "elegant" styles, and changes in the variety of demand do not occur easily. Consequently, the price of prefab houses stays high in order to create the fantasy of diversity.

It was in 2005 that I got a phone call from the developer of Soleil Project, who expressed doubts about the current housing situation. At the time a major

apparel company, Fast Retailing, had just made a price breakthrough for t-shirts and sweaters under the Uniqlo brand by means of a cheap system of production based in China. They told me that the price of house construction in Japan was too high, and that significant cost cutting could not be achieved even with mass production as long as it was based in Japan. So they decided they would locate their factory in Thailand and asked me to design the production system from the ground up. I was instinctively attracted to this request because I felt that diversity could be achieved by mass production. It doesn't mean I am against the strategy of house builders. Though it sounds contradictory to achieve diversity by making a large number of the same product, I had an inkling that this might be the right idea. Mass production does not just make diversity disappear, it also expands consumer choice, as long as there is a desire to mass produce everything thoroughly. I sought to emulate the role Uniqlo played in the retailing industry. I think it is possible for the Japanese house builder to increase diversity by restructuring the system of production and distribution so that they can produce new categories of housing. It cannot be done by making small design changes or adding functions.

Once I had agreed to the offer, we held a few meetings and decided on a rough scheme. It was a requirement that we use existing technologies as much as possible to save on the initial investment in the project. For the mass produced frame we decided to use the size of an existing sea transportation container, a 40-foot high cube. This made it possible to transport the unit with a container ship, keeping the marine transportation cost to a minimum. The format of the size of the trailer had been already established for road transportation in Japan. There was no reason to object to these limitations. Although the external size of the frame is about 2.4m × 12m × 2.9m, this size is not suitable for a residence, since the usable space further decreases when the space of the passage and the balcony are subtracted. Therefore, we planned to connect two or more frames, and it was necessary to consider a structure without any bracing. The structural engineer Jun Sato solved this problem by combining the directions of structural steel with a weak axis and a strong axis.

Because of Japanese traffic conditions, with their narrow roads, and the adaptation to a factory assembly line, we found it important not only to connect each frame but also to divide them. We manipulated the speed of production with the number of lines because the speed differed between frames with

plumbing and frames without. So we produced each frame separately and joined them at the end. Finally, with the frames finished on the interior at the factory in Thailand, they were shipped across the sea to the port in Japan. After the frames were carried to the site, ten frames could be assembled with marvellous speed in a single day. One building with 14 twin corridor type units and 5 floors was put up in 2 weeks. The height of five stories had been determined by Japanese regulations and for structural reasons. Within that height restriction, we assembled the stairs or elevator shaft with a combination of production in the Thai factory and some on-site assembly in Japan.

Metabolist architects tried to plan updates by clearly distinguishing the trunk and the minor parts of the building, but the social and performance deterioration of the trunk did not permit the update of the minor parts. This time, even the core is made with prefabrication, without any trunks. This is expected to bring architectural updating to a new dimension.

After one year on the project, I got a commission from a major housing developer. This developer collaborates with the architect on product development. I am not required to get hands on the sales system etc. in this

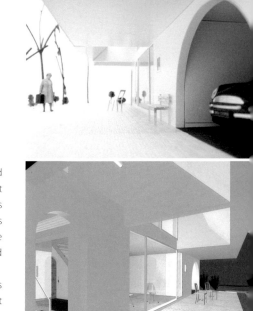

proposal, just to participate in the design. The form has not been influenced by restrictions of construction matters. I was interested by the developer's next theme, the "100 Years" housing type. It is quite unusual to think that developers might increase their profit by lengthening the life span of the house, which is normally about 30 years. One concern is a fear of short-term financial loss, while there is also the possibility of a house losing its character when mass-produced with long-lasting materials.

Though it is not unheard of that one's house might last for 100 years, it is sure to bring substantial change to consumer choice if all of the houses built by a developer are guaranteed to last that long. It would bring change not only to people's way of thinking about purchasing a house; it would also change the ratio of disposable income that can be spent on other consumption. The change is sure to increase the quality of life.

The 100 Years project secures diversity by longevity, while the theme of the Soleil Project is securing diversity by quantity. We grappled with two projects having seemingly contradictory themes. It raises the issue of how to confront the current state of the house, which cannot last for 100 years even if it is built solidly and can be updated.

We started by researching what the climate in Japan will be 100 years from now. The Center of Climate Research at Tokyo University estimates the temperature in Japan in 100 years will be 4 – 6 degrees Celsius higher than today. The Intergovernmental Panel on Climate Change has the same expectation. It will cause the number of hot summer days to double, while the number of heavy rainfall days will increase by the same amount. The future house is supposed to correspond to this climate in order to last 100 years. It does not make any sense to last that long, even if the house is tough and renewable, if people cannot live safely in it. We think that if the house becomes easier for people to live in as time goes by, the house could be kept for 100 years.

Traditionally, people in Japan strongly support south-facing houses, and we often see housing advertisements with a big open window toward the south. However, because the heat has intensified with global warming, this tendency is no longer suitable. Besides, most Japanese lots do not have enough distance from the road, which is why the windows tend to be covered with a curtain to protect privacy. This was a big point in our reconsideration of the design.

The house that we proposed turns to the north. This house opens to the north and shuts to the south, in order to deal with global warming, much as penguins survive in the South Pole. Sunshine is taken from the slit at the rooftop. According to the latitude of Japan, the angle of the roof of this house intercepts the strong sun in summer, while the winter sun is invited to the back

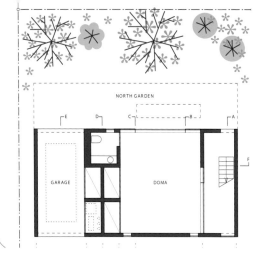

NORTH GARDEN

E   D   C   B   A

F

GARAGE

DOMA

STORAGE

LIVING

BED ROOM

DINING

BATH

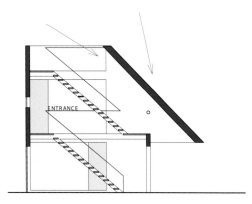

ENTRANCE

SECTION A

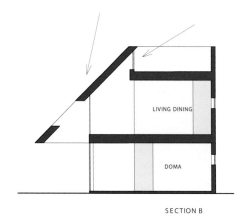

LIVING DINING

DOMA

SECTION B

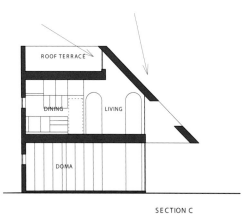

ROOF TERRACE

DINING   LIVING

DOMA

SECTION C

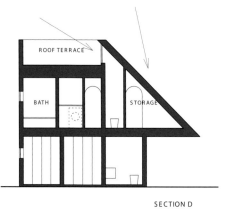

ROOF TERRACE

BATH   STORAGE

SECTION D

of the living room. The roof makes a big space under the eaves, so people can enjoy a rainy day in this house. The garden can have a lot of sunlight because the sharp angle of the roof delivers enough light there, where people can enjoy gardening. Moreover, because steady light from the north is suitable for uses such as ateliers, the first floor is assumed to be *doma*, the indoor-outdoor area in traditional Japanese houses. (Usually, there is no space where shoes are worn inside Japanese houses.) While the placement of the house should inevitably come near to the south of the lot, it has a large rooftop, disregarding the law that limits height from the north side of the road.

In this way I became committed to two mass-production projects. It has been a long time since consumers' sense of values has shifted from favouring quantity of diversity to quality of diversity. The common basis of these two projects is that we do not have to choose between diversity and quality, a choice that has had a bad influence on Japanese living space. Although these projects are not yet built, I have begun solving the problem. I am taking on these tough commissions and hope to show results in the near future.

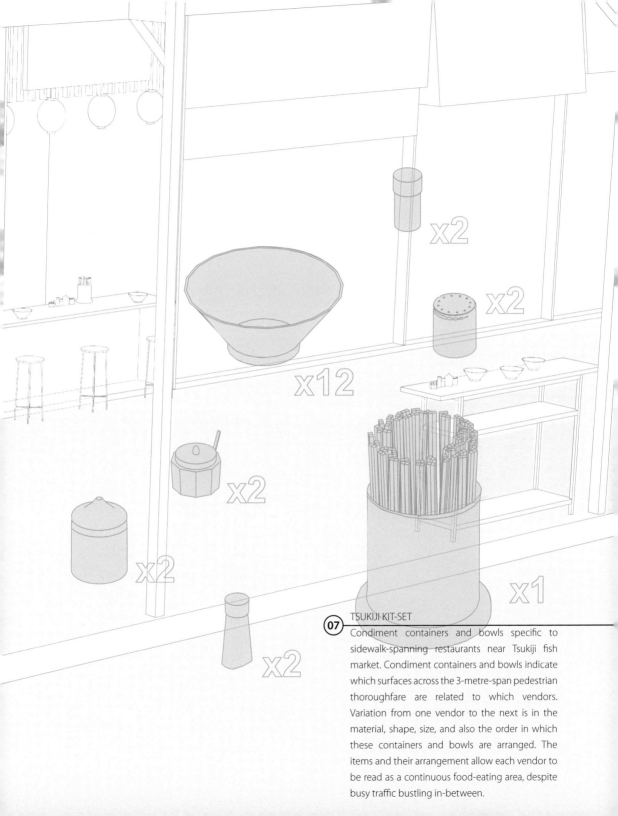

x2

x2

x2

x12

x2

x2

x1

x2

TSUKIJI KIT-SET

07 Condiment containers and bowls specific to sidewalk-spanning restaurants near Tsukiji fish market. Condiment containers and bowls indicate which surfaces across the 3-metre-span pedestrian thoroughfare are related to which vendors. Variation from one vendor to the next is in the material, shape, size, and also the order in which these containers and bowls are arranged. The items and their arrangement allow each vendor to be read as a continuous food-eating area, despite busy traffic bustling in-between.

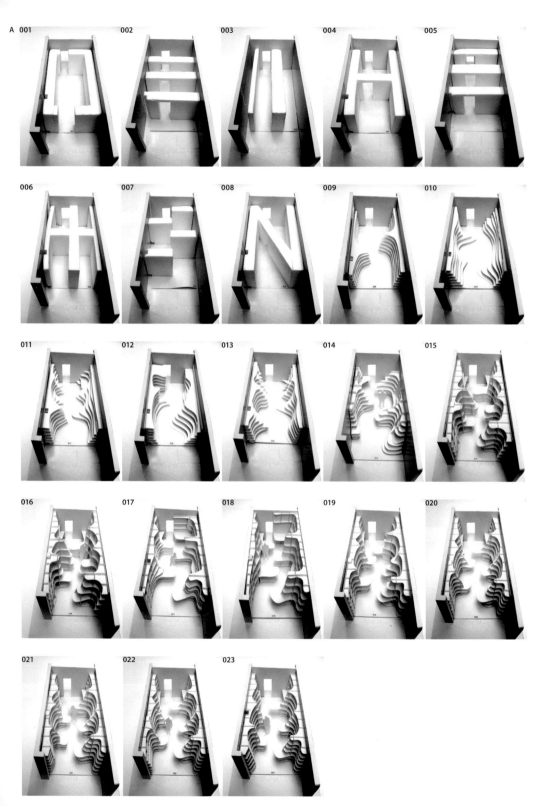

Super Linear Design Process Theory
Towards New Contextualism

RYUJI FUJIMURA

Designing With Linear Processes

If we were to examine the conceptual origins of OMA's 2004 Casa da Musica, we would need to go back four years earlier, to Rotterdam and a small project called Y2K. It has been well documented that this sculptural shape and unique composition, first developed for this single-family home but never realized, came to light later on and was directly appropriated for Porto's large concert hall. The leap is a crucial one. In general, architects' projects are explained in a very linear manner following their completion. They are portrayed as if they had been designed using processes just as linear, even though by nature it is quite fragmentary. In spite of this fact, the true, inherently non-linear nature of the design process is often kept camouflaged. However, in the case of Koolhaas' Casa da Musica, not only did he remove the camouflage but even proclaimed the fact publicly. It is for this reason that Koolhaas' particular stance here is not only mischievous but one quite meaningful and worth further examination. It leads us to ask, if we are talking about an approach to design, what might be the contrasting position?

Differing drastically from a system of trace-paper overlay, where ideas are continuously redrawn from their starting point, the use of CAD software now enables the designer to produce and present an infinitely large number of architectural schemes. This increase in amount allows not only for great expansion in choice, but also for continuous before/after comparisons. How, then, can this issue of infinite quantity be managed and practically applied to the design process? What I would like to discuss here is the possibility of redefining a design process as one that is perfectly iterative: a "super linear" design process. The paradox lies in the possibility that logic itself can be transcended through the continuous repetition of a logical procedure.

1. Actual architect, or architect in reality - Non-Linear
2. Ideal architect or architect in logic - Linear
3. Virtual architect or architect in literal way - Super Linear

Two Cases: Utsawa and K-Project

To demonstrate the above, I would like to introduce two cases. The first is a project for the Utsawa tableware shop, a 30-square-metre space located in

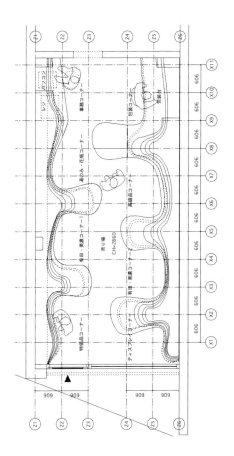

the suburbs of Tokyo. According to the owner's experienced opinion that if customers remain longer in the shop, then sales would increase, the design of a serpentine traffic line in a single track was introduced. This arrangement also allowed for the display of various categories of tableware, including western-style, Japanese traditional, special-priced, and exclusive items.

Design development began first with a simple volumetric study. Shelf depth and passage width were picked up as temporary clues, and from this several variations were tentatively produced, such as the ordinary enclosure type (A-001), layer type (A-002), line type (A-003), H type (A-004), depth emphasis type (A-005), fine type (A-006), zigzag type (A-007), perspective emphasis type (A-008), and so on.

After this initial trial, the owner made the request that for administrative reasons, a single room was preferred over a subdivided space. Thus one room became the rule for the remainder of the study. Shelves were then arranged on both side walls, while two projections were tentatively generated from left and right (A-009). Various patterns were subsequently tested (A-010 – A-013) until the desired rhythm for the projections had been achieved, at which point vertical boards were introduced (A-014).

Certain obvious rules began to appear, such as, the arc of the horizontal board's curve must meet the point of the vertical board (A-015), while the wavelength of the curve must remain in step with the span of the grid. Following this, further conditions were placed on the curve rhythm, the grid spacing, the layer of the curves as seen from the entrance, and so on until the final scheme was eventually realized (A-023).

Throughout the process, various rules regarding the overall form were picked up step by step. As a result, the scheme had become simultaneously endowed with a very logical progression as well as a leap of imagination. This iteration of a feedback design methodology was then similarly applied, in much larger scale and complexity, to K-Project.

K-Project is a 1,500-square-metre building complex located in a Tokyo residential area, consisting of both shops and residences. At first glance it appears like several volumes floating on top of one large ground floor plate. Even if the external volume appears composed at random, it also tries to maintain an aesthetic simplicity, especially in contrast to its internal intricacy. For example, at street level, the shop space is designed to be without columns. And at the fifth floor level, from a 900mm mega-beam hangs the second, third, and fourth stories, supported by four integrated equipment cores. Other important — if even less visible — components of the project are to include in the budget accrued maintenance costs, and to improve sustainability of construction by choosing responsible equipment and structural systems.

Design work began, as with Utsawa, from a simple rectangular volume, and the super linear design method was adopted. First, the maximum capacity was taken, and a shape with an uncomplicated structure was chosen (B-001). Though both steel and reinforced concrete structures were examined (B-002 – B-006), steel was ultimately selected at an early stage, due to the site's traffic restrictions and the expected savings in construction cost. Since it had been decided early in the business plan to have only residences above the ground floor level, a simple volume was placed on top of the shop volume (B-007).

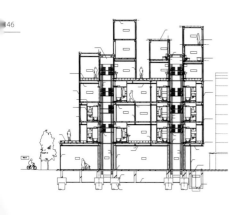

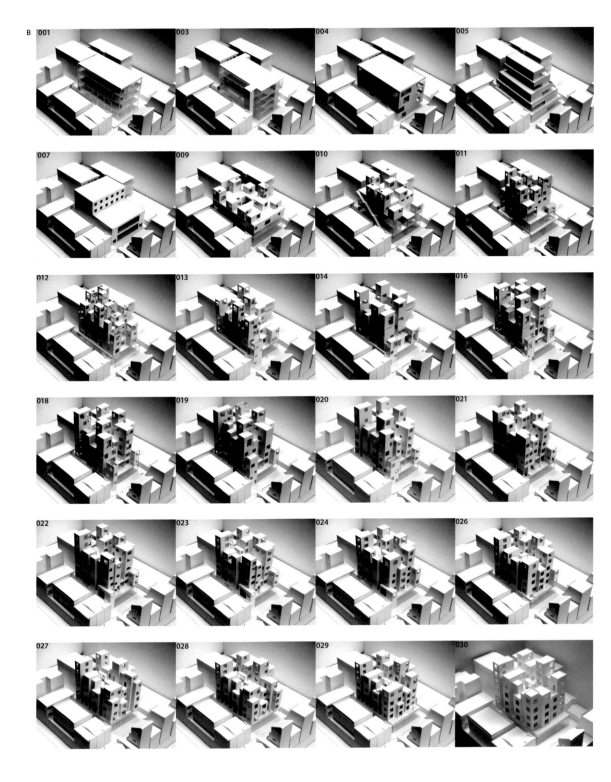

Individual gardens were created by subdividing this residential volume as though they were detached houses, allowing for a fully functional roof level (B-009). Then, since it seemed unnatural to have rooftop gardens without any relation to the shopping street, the volume on one side was cut down slightly (B-010). Since some of the volume's verticality had been lost, the lines in the corners were then emphasized (B-011, B-012). At that stage, the design work was inspired by the high-density, energetic apartment complexes in the Hong Kong downtown.

As the arrangement gradually moved towards an executable scheme, the first responsibility was to establish the vertical equipment spaces. Among the random volumes, adjoining corners were brought to touch, and extended from top to bottom as equipment cores (B-016). They were then brought to the outside of the volume, where it was necessary to include not only water supply and drainage but also exhaust openings, boiler, and outdoor air-conditioning equipment. The design then proceeded to emphasize the vertical lines in elevation by lining up the towers along the shop-volume platform (B-019).

After repeated examinations of an appropriate structural system, and faced with the uneconomical option of having structure appear independently in each of the towers, a mega-structure was decided upon (B-022). From there, this system consolidated around the already established equipment spaces. As the structural scheme developed, the final shape of the volumes began to solidify at the same time (B-023 – B-028). One final condition — that the windows occurring in each tower volume be aligned — was added at the end (B-030), and the final schematic design was reached at that point.

The Simultaneous Progress of Research and Design

Such a design process appears normal but it contains two important differences. One is that the feedback of new information is methodically repeated with each step along the way. Here, the idea in question is criticized immediately and is fed back directly and without bias into the succeeding idea, avoiding any combination with unrelated ideas, or transferring altogether to a quite different idea. As a result, because the outcome was obtained by processing innumerable feedbacks, the design process can be said to become completely logical in its intention.

The other difference is that the specific way the design deals with the program and site in question has been acquired heuristically, or by trial and error. The thought behind this is to allow the research and the design process an opportunity to occur at a simultaneous rate, rather than simply reflecting the cumulative result of the research in a final design. By referring, for example, to the boundary conditions of the shapes and their adoption process, this intention might be better understood.

In K-Project, a total of 21 items were identified during the design process. By starting from negotiating general matters such as capacity and structure, the processing and implementation of practical issues — such as building regulations, planning, cost, structure, and technical equipment — are gradually added at later stages of design development. It is at this point, importantly, that most of the design process was spent addressing these concerns. Before that, up to about step no. 30, the work was focused primarily on making the design parameters rise to the surface. Once the boundary condition had been confirmed, comparative studies could be made freely, now that certain parameters were already in place. For the final steps, tasks became still more specific: for example, seeking a more beautiful shape, or negotiating with neighbourhood residents regarding decreasing the number of stories while maintaining the same floor area.

Here, all steps occurring before the final boundary condition were finalized are seen as the "searching process," and those occurring after, the "comparative process." Although it is part of the same overall design, the purpose of the work is much different, as it is adjusting the condition along the way, and confirming its balance as a whole.

Towards New Contextualism

By using a system of feedback, the physical conditions of form are being continuously updated and clarified. This way of setting parameters, without simplifying what is an innately complex condition, allows the preceding result to be input immediately into the next idea. Not unlike the metaphor of a computer algorithm, realistically this means that both a large amount of ideas can be explored, and from them simple conclusions can be repeatedly output. The purpose, however, is by no means to simply imitate the computer. Indeed, the computer has inherent structural features that are simply better equipped for certain specificities of an architecture project such as managing building regulations, structure, equipment, cost, and so on.

As someone who grew up in a typical, new suburban town, a thin space made of steel structure and decorated with endless signage is too routine to resist. But at some point I came to believe it is necessary to investigate alternate ways to approach the building process and to form a sound basis on which design may relate directly to the power of a particular place. Moreover, could architecture strive to build persuasively and justly in the here and now, without falling, like the postmodernists did, into acts of mere symbolism? A growing awareness of such issues became my motive for pursuing this type of "super linear" thinking.

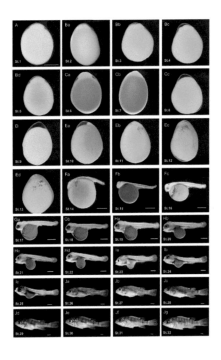

Lawrence Lessig, in his analysis of modern power in contemporary society, isolates four main types: law, norm, market, and architecture. Though such types of power are invisible in the early stage of design, they become visible through the act of building architecture. With this in mind, is it then possible to establish a new means of design by introducing the element of time into our view of architecture? Can the developmental staging process of the fish, in its acceptance of external environmental mechanisms, be used as an analogical example? The most important goal for architects in our contemporary society is to establish the image of "new design" by redefining architecture from its very foundation, so to compete in a world changing due to the powers of economy and information. It has therefore become necessary to use computerization in the design process in order to achieve smart, beautiful architecture, to improve efficiency in collaboration, and to restructure the urban landscape overrun by homogenization. In such a context, designing "new forms" or "new space" is quite a superficial pursuit for society. What, then, is modern "new design"? What is its social meaning and future potential? The "super linear" design process shown here is one such theoretical proposal, envisioning a new image for architecture, and aiming to increase fruitful practice and discussion.

Dialogue: Koji Aoki + Ryuji Fujimura
Design Method of Japanese Architects after SANAA

KOJI AOKI + RYUJI FUJIMURA

This is a record of an email dialogue between two young architects — both born in 1976 — currently based in Tokyo. Koji Aoki has been working in the office of Sou Fujimoto.[1] Ryuji Fujimura has been studying under Yoshiharu Tsukamoto at Tokyo Institute of Technology (Atelier Bow-wow)[2] and running his own firm.[3] The discussion is about the young generation of Japanese architects after SANAA (Kazuyo Sejima[4] and Ryue Nishizawa[5]).

Fig. 1, Study of Treatment Center for Mentally Disturbed Children

Fig. 2, 21st Century Museum of Contemporary Art, Kanazawa

From: Koji Aoki
Date: 2007.1.22 10:38 PM
Fujimura,

Good evening, this is Aoki from the Sou Fujimoto office.
The situation of young Japanese architects today is difficult. For me, Sejima's diagrammatic design method carries great conviction, not only because of its formal sophistication, but also its structural and material refinement. While the work might sometimes seem overly simplified and diagrammatic, it represents a unique and very real achievement. On the other hand, there are some ways in which its influence has been negative. Some young architects don't nurture the diagram or shape carefully, leaving the impression that shape itself is the only achievement of the work.

Anyway, after SANAA, I think there is a tendency for many young architects to be very self conscious about form in a way that produces building as diagram. It is even possible to now sort this work out and organize it by its specific patterns and characteristics.

[1] Diagram → Architecture : SANAA, Sou Fujimoto, Akihisa Hirata[6]

[2] Diagram → Device : Yuko Nagayama[7]

[3] Diagram → Character : Hiroshi Nakamura,[8] Takeshi Hosaka,[9] and others

Well, this is my first pass at this break down. To clarify it further, I hand the discussion over to you!

From: Ryuji Fujimura
Date: 2007.1.24 11:55 PM
Aoki,

This is Fujimura. Let's begin with a big statement:

The recent completion of SANAA's 21st Century Museum of Contemporary Art in Kanazawa in 2004, and Jun Aoki's[10] Aomori Prefectural Museum in 2006, has offered up two projects that can be used to illustrate essential paradigms that now characterize contemporary Japanese architecture. (It should go without saying that both were highly influenced by Rem Koolhaas)

SANAA in Kanazawa: PLAN: DIAGRAM: THE NETHERLANDS IN THE 1990s [Fig. 2]

Jun Aoki in Aomori: LANGUAGE: NARRATIVE: ARCHITECTURAL ASSOCIATION IN THE 1980s [Fig. 3]

I think that recent discussions in Japan by the younger generation of architects can also be understood in the suggested boundaries of this framing. So the question at hand is to doubt the frame itself.

For instance, in another model, the architect's problem in contemporary society is laid out by sociologist Shinji Miyadai in *City Where We Want to Live* (edited by Riken Yamamoto in 2006). Miyadai's model employs the analogy of layers, framing surface against depth:

Surface: FREE, SUPERFICIAL, ICONOGRAPHY, JOKES: ARCHITECTURE

Depth: INFRASTRUCTURE, SYSTEMS, WASTE, MAGNITUDE

Briefly put, the terms of reference that architects use, such as diagram, space, or character actually are only trifling events on the surface layer. In this context, Miyadai's criticism poses that architects' proposals have no more meaning — or effect — than that of simple amusement.

Arata Isozaki has objected to Miyadai, saying that even if architects are not producing significant built works, they will continually advance the discourse towards the future, and they are still working as architects. It is possible to take just a defiant attitude, but Isozaki's intention appeared clearly in "Gifu Kitagata Apartment, North Block, First Phase" (*Shinkenchiku*, June 2006 issue).

On the other hand, I am anxious about Fujimoto's recent comment saying that "For me, a social problem or global capitalism or something like that is such a tiny thing" (The dialogue with Junya Ishigami, Oki Sato in *Shinkenchiku Jutaku Tokusyu* January 2007 issue) because he always pretends to be unconscious about the relationship between architecture and society. Space is framed as if it was the antidote of society or the last bastion for the architect. It could be offered that the reason why young Japanese architects do not make space is that the world has been *de-spatialized*. How do you object if it is true?

From: Koji Aoki
Date: 2007.1.26 10:25 PM

Fujimura,

Thanks for your reply. This is Aoki.

Are you suggesting that by energizing layers or *surface* and *depth*, architects can set a social agenda for architecture and then somehow avoid collapsing into fancy, formal ideas? So, maybe you want to ask the architect what he thinks he's doing, just playing with space without considering such social propositions?

I believe that SANAA and Fujimoto are not simply amusing themselves, but in fact trying to extend architecture's life by producing architectural form that might connect in meaningful ways to the public. It's healthy for contemporary architects to seek a reconciliation with the public, to bridge between *this side* and *that side*.

It is a problem to abandon the cause of making a connection to society and focus only on autonomous architectural expression. I think the circular and insider discussion about design technique itself is not meaningful — as was demonstrated by Jun Aoki and Ryue Nishizawa's dialogue in *Shinkenchiku* (September 2006 issue). It was just another confirmation of their focus on formal expression.

Even if it sounds old fashioned, there is a risk that the potential of the building program might be left unexploited, as the agenda of architects standing on *this side*, try to resuscitate architecture by focusing on the formalization of *space*. Can *space*, dematerialized and abstracted by architects obsessed with the interior logic of their work, be meaningful today to a polarized and disaffected public?

Anyway, I don't think that we need to oppose the values and practices of the previous generation, but it is our responsibility to critically engage their work as the generation that follows them. At the same time, it's clear that our generation of architects in Japan does not share a single consciousness, or operate as one community. We are pointing in different directions, and amusing ourselves in different ways.

Where do you stand as an architect now?

From: Ryuji Fujimura
Date: 2007.2.1 8:31 PM

Aoki,

The way you describe the generations recalls what happened in the middle of the 1990s when there was a community called "the conference of 100 architects in their 30s." Toyo Ito recently named it *Sazanami* (ripple) *Architects*.

I think the reason why the younger generation in Japan seems to amuse themselves is because one half is aligned with the older generation while the other half connects to its own age group. They don't take time to share opinions with each other.

On the other hand, there is peculiar heat to the discussion within this generation, and it is personally interesting as a movement, not just journalism. Recently, we've discussed the conceptual model that juxtaposes the relations between the surface and depth of the architectural object.

For me, Hiroya Tanaka's[11] opinion was interesting. He said, "Only through spatial representation can the essential conventions be criticized and influenced. Therefore, only the work that clearly represents the image of an unprecedented future world can galvanize the next generation."

I would argue that the competition between ideas — as represented by images — is not the most important consideration, because architecture is not defined by images alone. As an over simplification, it recalls the way Cecil Balmond uses the concept of the *algorithm* as a tool for defining qualities for small, programmatically simple projects. The challenge is to understand how something as specific as an algorithm might be applied to determine something as complex as a housing project in the middle of a city.

But I do think there could be meaningful attempts to discover and explore algorithmic codes in real urban space. For instance, in studying the organization of *supermarkets*, I realized that the section of their interiors are divided into two zones. The upper part of it is used for signs, and the lower part is dedicated to flows of products and people. This arrangement corresponds to the basic physiology of the human body — *eyes above* and *feet below*. Similar organizations exist in airports, terminal stations, large plazas, and highways. It is interesting that those binary conditions are analogically similar to computers, which consist of desktop (the visual) and database (the workings). And the same kind of polarization can be found in our everyday life, where the city is an information system and architecture is a piece of contrived and isolated design.

I suppose that the *supermarket* is the perfect analog of the information system theory of urban space, while *model*, with the implication of autonomy,

Fig. 3, Aomori Museum of Art

idealization and simulation is currently effective for architectural theory.

It could be argued that SANAA initiated a new architecture predicated on the formal authority and closure of the model. Fujimoto added to the discretion of the model, the suggestion of an algorithmic design, a way of thinking process that challenged the specificity of form. In that sense, Junya Ishigami[12] escalates Fujimoto's algorithmic design method further. In his latest work, The Atelier of Kanagawa Institute of Technology (2007), over 300 steel columns rotate freely within the space [Fig. 4].

The studios of SANAA, Sou Fujimoto, and Junya Ishigami rely heavily on student interns, and their presence has made these offices into factories for model production. The actual staff of these firms is outnumbered and visually erased by the new landscape — *scenery of interns*.

What do you think of this new flow of volunteers?

From: Koji Aoki
Date: 2007.2.6 8:15 PM

Fujimura,

Good evening, this is Aoki.

The *scenery of interns* is certainly spreading. On the other hand, when I talked with Hiroshi Kikuchi[13] before, I sensed the emergence of an alternative when he said, "only one model was made during the design process, because every part was checked with CG."

There seem to be two methods now. In the first, there is a seminal initial image, followed by convergence of all the fragments of study. This would be Method A (example: Toyo Ito). The other one generates the structure not by having a clear image at the outset, but by stacking small solutions. This is Method B (example: Kazuyo Sejima).

Models are used in [A], but in a role similar to CG. It is like the confirmation work, justifying a destination identified at the start. [B] is a method that shows models have to be produced in quantity in order to approach the design of the whole. In general, it is hard to find either has amazing speed, or the feeling of scale in model study because it is a manual work. If a similar process can be traced by information technology, it would be possible to handle the scale more fictitiously, I guess. However, have you ever seen the space that is the product of such a design act? Even if Shohei Matsukawa[14] introduces the spec of such strong arms, I do not think that he masters it in his work.

The form of Sou Fujimoto's Treatment Center for Mentally Disturbed Children [Fig. 5] is the product of the manual study of a group of quite similar models. Its form is very specific and could not easily be duplicated or applied to other problems. I think Junya Ishigami's work avoids the trap of producing the building's structure through the willful surplus of identical parts, even if the reason for the specificity cannot finally be honestly understood.

From: Ryuji Fujimura
Date: 2007.2.24 3:52 PM
Aoki,

This is Fujimura.

Up to now, Aoki has focused on *space*, and I seem to be speaking about *design*. We do not doubt the importance of *space* and perhaps, are not doubting the existence of its structure — or the *metaspace* that is behind the composition. In the works of Kazuyo Sejima, Ryue Nishizawa, Sou Fujimoto, or Junya Ishigami — around whom our discussion revolves — there is both *space* and *metaspace* and the synthesis of the two is what we think might be *design*. It is agreed that *model*, the *scenery of interns*, and *computer algorithm* might constitute some of the mediation tools between two spaces.

In contrast, the works of Yuko Nagayama or Hiroshi Nakamura cannot be evaluated with the same critical terms of reference, because their work always follows the logic of materials and construction methods. I think that there is a big difference in this work, even if in the end, it talks to the same young generation. The method we are currently confirming is discovering *metaspace* in the design process and the assignment we are challenging is how the *metaspace* is richly related to *space*.

I think that Toyo Ito's "Strong Thing," Riken Yamamoto's "System," Jun Aoki's "Decision rule," Shohei Matsukawa's "Function space," or even Seikun Kikutake's "Changing things and unchanging things" are all indicating the same form of design.

Fig. 4, Atelier of Kanagawa Institute of Technology

Fig. 5, Treatment Center for Mentally Disturbed Children

From: Koji Aoki
Date: 2007.2.27 0:36 AM

Fujimura,

Good evening, this is Aoki.

In the design process of Fujimoto's Treatment Center for Mentally Disturbed Children, after hitting on the image of the scattered box [Fig. 6], the spatial matter and functional zoning was inspired precisely through the method of layering the sketch on the model photograph, while moving the small box made of styrofoam little by little [Fig. 1]. This is a reaction from my personal experience. How do you arrange the *design process* we have been discussing up to now?

From: Ryuji Fujimura
Date: 2007.3.1 7:50 PM
Aoki,

This is Fujimura.

The difference of the substance between *diagram* and *narrative* becomes not so important. The difference of whether *metaspace* is to exist or to not exist, or whether to discover *metaspace* by algorithm or inspiration seems, on the other hand, significantly more important.

This time, we have discussed the design method of *formal*, *model-like* and *searching* as distinct from the methods of *improvisation*, *CG-like* and *imagination*. It tries to seek a new design method between the method of a great master's sketch and the one of a computer algorithm. I think it must be a meaningful discussion.

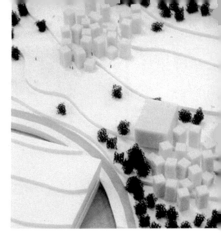

Fig. 6, Study of Treatment Center for Mentally Disturbed Children

Koji Aoki: Architect born in 1976. Since graduating from Muroran Institute of Technology, has worked for Sou Fujimoto Architects. Dormitory (2003) and Treatment Center for Mentally Disturbed Children (2006), Tokyo Apartments (2008)

Ryuji Fujimura: Architect based in Tokyo Japan. Born in 1976. Studied at the Berlage-Institue, Rotterdam, the Netherlands in 2002 – 2003. Established Ryuji Fujimura Architects in 2005. Doctoral Researcher in Tokyo Institute of Technology, Yoshiharu Tsukamoto Laboratory. [www.ryujifujimura.jp]

[1]Sou Fujimoto (1971 –) [http://www.sou-fujimoto.com]
[2]Yoshiharu Tsukamoto (1965 –) [http://www.bow-wow.jp]
[3]Ryuji Fujimura (1976 –) [http://www.ryujifujimura.jp]
[4]Kazuyo Sejima (1956 –) [http://www.sanaa.co.jp]
[5]Ryue Nishizawa (1966 –) [http://www.sanaa.co.jp]
[6]Akihisa Hirata (1975 –) [http://www.hao.nu]
[7]Yuko Nagayama (1975 –) [http://www1.odn.ne.jp/yukon/index.html]
[8]Hiroshi Nakamura (1972 –) [http://www.hao.nu]
[9]Takeshi Hosaka (1975 –) [http://www.hosakatakeshi.com]
[10]Jun Aoki (1956 –) [http://www.aokijun.com]
[11]Hiroya Tanaka (1975 –)
[12]Junya Ishigami (1974 –)
[13]Hiroshi Kikuchi (1972 –) [http://www.hiroshikikuchi.com]
[14]Shohei Matsukawa (1974 –) [http://www.000studio.com]

Fig. 1, Study of Treatment Center for Mentally Disturbed Children
(2006, Sou Fujimoto) in "Searching Process" © Sou Fujimoto Architects
Fig. 2, 21st Century Museum of Contemporary Art, Kanazawa (2004, SANAA)
Fig. 3, Aomori Museum of Art (2006, Jun Aoki)
Fig. 4, Atelier of Kanagawa Institute of Technology (2007, Junya Ishigami)
Fig. 5, Treatment Center for Mentally Disturbed Children (2006, Sou Fujimoto)
© Sou Fujimoto Architects
Fig. 6, Study of Treatment Center for Mentally Disturbed Children
(2006, Sou Fujimoto) in "Comparison Process" © Sou Fujimoto Architects

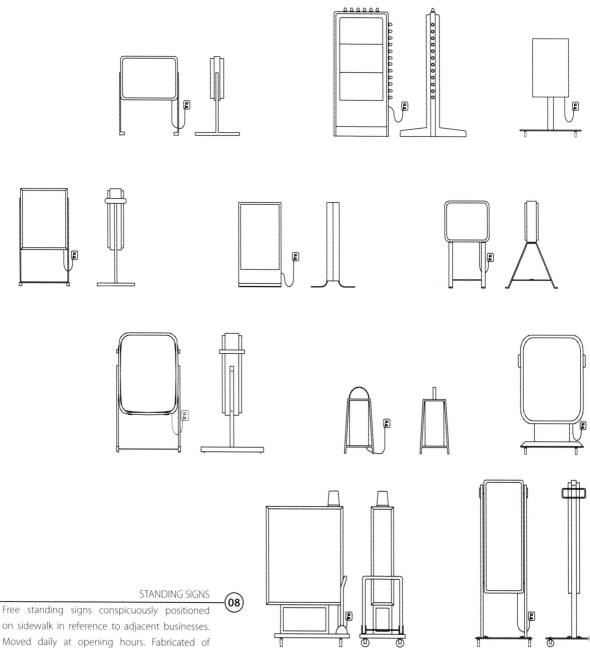

STANDING SIGNS

Free standing signs conspicuously positioned on sidewalk in reference to adjacent businesses. Moved daily at opening hours. Fabricated of aluminum, steel and plastic. Standing 65cm – 185cm tall. Electric-powered media: backlit plastic and flashing bulbs.

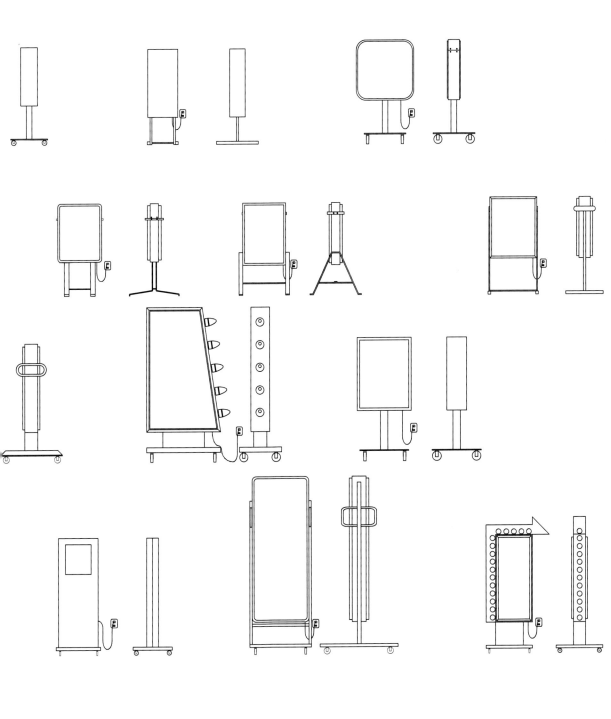

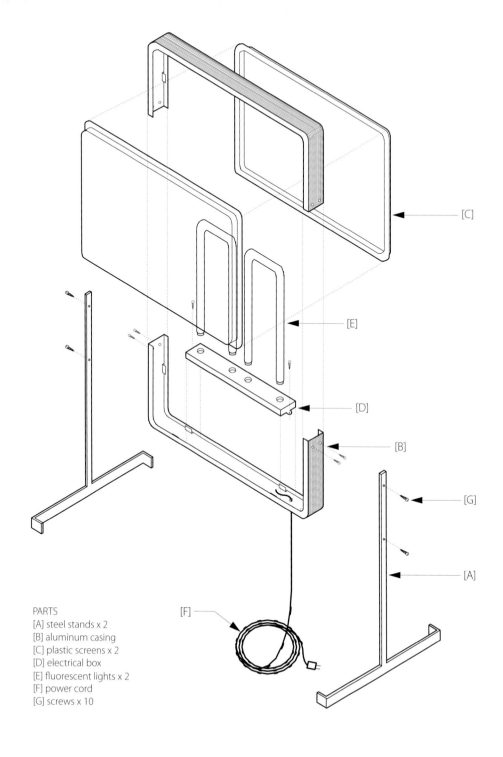

[C]

[E]

[D]

[B]

[G]

[A]

PARTS
[A] steel stands x 2
[B] aluminum casing
[C] plastic screens x 2
[D] electrical box
[E] fluorescent lights x 2
[F] power cord
[G] screws x 10

[F]

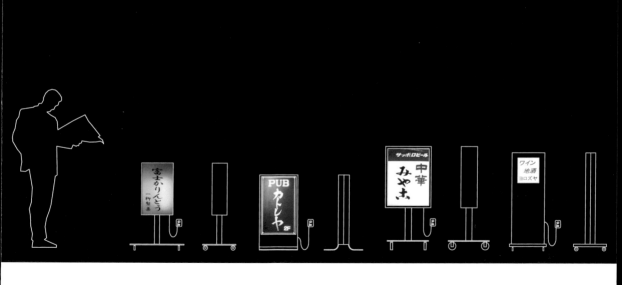

PHOTO CREDITS

apartment 1

12, 13, 14, 15, 16, 17, 19, 21, 23, 24 © Daichi Ono

25 © George Wagner

7[+1] Works

30 – 61 © Sou Fujimoto Architects

Practical Aspects of a Space of Invention

70, 72, 74, 84, 86, 87, 88, 90, 91, 92, 93 © Koji Taki

71, 75, 77 © Atsushi Aiba

77 (middle) © David Zeibin

Platform

98, 101, 103, 105, 107, 108, 110 © Masao Nishikawa

100 © David Zeibin

Build

117, 118, 120, 121, 122, 123, 125 (lower right) © Toyo Ito & Associates, Architects

116, 119, 121 (lower right), 122 (lower left) © Nacasa and Partners

124, 125 © Oriol Rig

126, 127 © Christian Gahl

Diversity through Mass-Production

132, 134, 135, 136, 137, 138, 139, 141 © Yasutaka Yoshimura Architects

Super Linear Design Process Theory

144, 145, 146, 147, 148, 149 © Ryuji Fujimura Architects

Dialogue: Koji Aoki + Ryuji Fujimura

150, 159 (lower), 161 © Sou Fujimoto Architects

152 © SANAA

156 © Jun Aoki & Associates

159 © Junya Ishigama + Associates

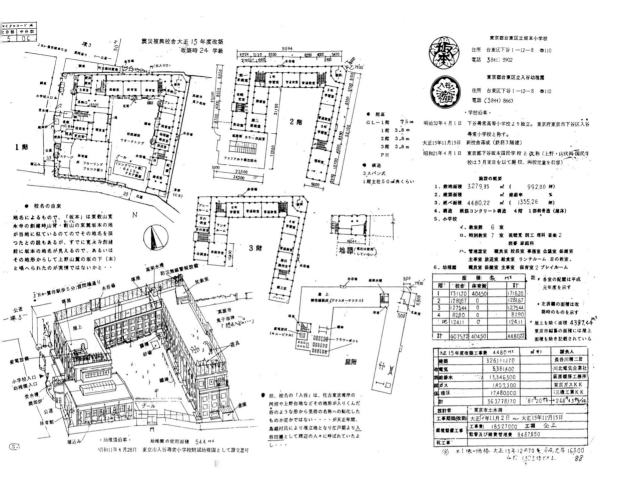

CONTRIBUTOR WEBSITES

Kumiko Inui www.inuiuni.com
Sou Fujimoto www.sou-fujimoto.com
John + Patricia Patkau www.patkau.ca
Manabu Chiba www.chibamanabu.jp
Yasutaka Yoshimura www.ysmr.com
Ryuji Fujimura www.ryujifujimura.jp